Total Business Planning

MODERN ACCOUNTING

PERSPECTIVES AND PRACTICE

Gary John Previts, Series Editor

PRACTICAL ACCOUNTING FOR LAWYERS
Robert O. Berger, Jr.

INDEPENDENT AUDITOR'S GUIDE TO OPERATIONAL
AUDITING
Dale L. Flesher and Stewart Siewert

AN ACCOUNTANT'S GUIDE TO COMPUTER SYSTEMS
William E. Perry

QUALITY CONTROL AND PEER REVIEW
James W. Pattillo

CPA LIABILITY
Jonathan Davies

EDP CONTROLS: A GUIDE FOR AUDITORS AND
ACCOUNTANTS
Martin B. Roberts

ACCOUNTING: HOW TO MEET THE CHALLENGES OF
RELEVANCE AND REGULATION
Eugene H. Flegm

THE SCOPE OF CPA SERVICES: A STUDY OF THE DEVELOPMENT
OF THE CONCEPT OF INDEPENDENCE AND THE PROFESSION'S
ROLE IN SOCIETY
Gary John Previts

TOTAL BUSINESS PLANNING: A STEP-BY-STEP
GUIDE WITH FORMS
E. James Burton and W. Blan McBride

Total Business Planning:
A Step-by-Step Guide with Forms

E. James Burton, Ph.D.
W. Blan McBride

Professional Growth Associates, Inc.
Tallahassee, Florida

WILEY

John Wiley & Sons
New York • Chichester • Brisbane • Toronto • Singapore

Library of Congress Cataloging in Publication Data:

Burton, E. James.

Total business planning: a step-by-step guide with forms /
E. James Burton, W. Blan McBride.

p.   cm. — (Modern accounting perspectives and practice)
Bibliography: p.
ISBN 0-471-82379-1
1. Corporate planning.   I. McBride, W. Blan.   II. Title.
III. Series: Modern accounting perspectives and practice series.

HD30.28.B84   1988   658.4'012—dc19   87-28581 CIP
ISBN 0-471-82379-1

Printed in the United States of America

10 9 8 7 6 5 4 3 2

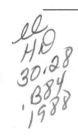
Contents

Preface   vii

Introduction   1

Using This Process   1

Frequently Asked Questions (with Answers) about Business
Planning   8

Business Planning Terms   12

The Document   13

The Planning Communications Process   19

Level 1   **Philosophy and Mission**   29

Level 2   **Strategic Plan**   43

Level 3   **Corporate Objectives**   53

Level 4   **Planning Unit Goals**   75

Level 5   **Tactics and Projections**   95

Level 6   **Coordination**   103

Appendix   113

Preface

This book is the product of the authors' personal experiences in leading thousands of planners in hundreds of seminars as well as leading scores of companies in the construction of their own business plans. It is compiled entirely from the authors' previously copyrighted seminar and other hands-on planning materials. It has one and only one objective: to assist you, the planning coordinator, in efficiently facilitating the building of more effective business plans for your organization.

The methodologies outlined in this book have been used successfully by the authors as well as by participants in their seminars in a multiplicity of industries and in businesses of every size. The methodologies have been successfully used to construct feasibility studies for new products, to construct short-term operating plans for units, to build plans aimed at the capital markets, for overall corporate operating plans, for strategic planning, and for business plans of all sorts and purposes.

If you use this book as a tool and you get the cooperation of the necessary persons in your organization, you will be able to build a business plan for your business. The book contains definitions, forms, and directions. It is necessary that you understand that the process outlined herein is not dependent upon the forms. The forms have been included for the purpose of making your job easier. Your objective is to draw the creative thinking out of the people in your organization, who will thereby gain a sense of commitment to making things happen.

The text pages intended for photocopying and distribution to others in the organization are indicated by a graphic* in the upper right-hand corner. The other pages give you, the planning coordinator, information and explanations. We have given examples of completed forms throughout the book. We caution you not to lean too heavily on these completed examples. These are intended only as thought provokers—use them as such. There is a complete set of blank forms in the appendix which you may photocopy and distribute as you need.

*

We have put this book together for you. It is simple and easy to use, and we wish you good planning with it.

We want to thank our wives and families for their patience with us as we worked on this book. And we want to say a special thank you to Mrs. Carol Corbett for her continuing efforts, her steady good humor, and her loyalty.

Also, we want to thank all of our clients. Our experiences working with you have contributed greatly to this book. There are too many of you to name without failing to mention someone. You know who you are, and so do we. Thank you!

E. JAMES BURTON, PH.D.
W. BLAN MCBRIDE

Total Business Planning

Introduction

USING THIS PROCESS

Obviously, there are many, varied types of organizations which want and need to create plans. The process described and forms provided in this book are effective for a wide range of organization types. On the following pages we will describe different scenarios of planning needs and how to use this book if your case is similar to one of these.

The scenarios we will describe are:

The small, start-up business

The small, ongoing, single-product business

The larger, limited-product business which is functionally divided (sales, marketing, production, administrative, etc.)

The larger, multiple-product business which is functionally divided

The large multiple-product business with largely autonomous divisions

The project or venture to be started within an existing business of any size

The not-for-profit entity.

We will also refer to and describe six **Levels** in the planning process:

1. Philosophy and Mission

2. Strategic Plan (Competitive Analysis)

3. Corporate Objectives

4. Planning Unit Goals

5. Tactics and Projections

6. Coordination

Each **Level** consists of multiple steps in the process; the term **Level** is used to break the continuous planning process into discrete parts. Individual action plans, accountabilities, and performance evaluations may be linked to appropriate levels in the planning process.

THE PLANNING PROCESS: 6 LEVELS

THE SMALL, START-UP BUSINESS

Two pitfalls trap more start-up businesses than any others: lack of adequate capital and lack of experience in the business. Even a mediocre business plan will help highlight these problems and the planner can either correct the deficiencies and proceed, or can postpone the venture until provisions are made.

In this case, the planning units are individuals and each individual may have several functions to cover. The organization chart probably looks like:

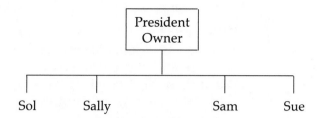

We recommend that a new venture focus its attention on:

Level 1 Philosophy and Mission
Level 2 Strategic Plan (Competitive Analysis)
Level 3 Corporate Objectives

Additional, thorough attention should be paid to these prospective financial matters: cash flow projections, pro forma balance sheet, and pro forma income statements.

Without diminishing the importance of **Levels 4** or **5** overall, the above describes the portions most helpful to the entrepreneur and most often initially requested by potential financing sources.

THE SMALL, ONGOING, SINGLE-PRODUCT BUSINESS

We assume that the key manager and/or owner of the business is active and participates in decisions throughout this type of business. The areas of the business are usually small and interact regularly and closely with each other. The organization chart may look like:

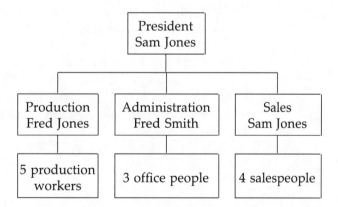

Because the business is small, it may not have distinct departments with managers over each. The planning units are quite possibly individuals. Therefore, **Levels 3** and **4** will merge into a single level where the corporate objectives are divided directly into action plans by people specifically assigned by top management. That is, the objectives are not separated into department goals, but rather the assigned person constructs an appropriate action plan from which individual accountabilities emerge. The department goals (**Level 4**) step is eliminated.

One plan covers the whole business because it isn't large enough for different agenda to have developed. And, there aren't enough resources to spread out over more projects.

THE LARGER, LIMITED-PRODUCT, FUNCTIONALLY DIVIDED BUSINESS

This is a classic scenario for using the total process described. The planning units are the functional areas, each of which has a key person at its head. While there may be more than one product, the company is probably geographically together and the organization chart may be similar to:

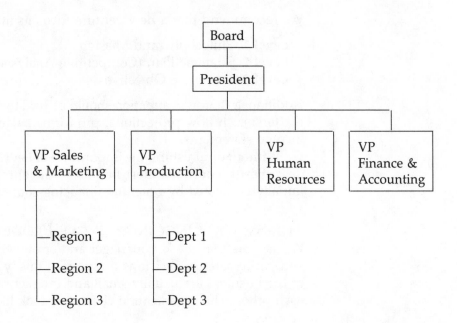

Because the vice-presidents are probably involved in **Levels 1** through **4**, our process should work very well. We recommend the full process in such cases. Corporate officers' accountabilities and performance evaluations are linked to every level in the process (**Levels 1** through **6**). Accountabilities and evaluations of departmental managers are linked to **Level 4** and **Level 5**, and those of individuals to **Level 5**. Communication of all pertinent parts of the plan is typically good and no large problems are likely.

The Larger, Multiple-Product, Functionally Divided Business

A typical organization chart might be:

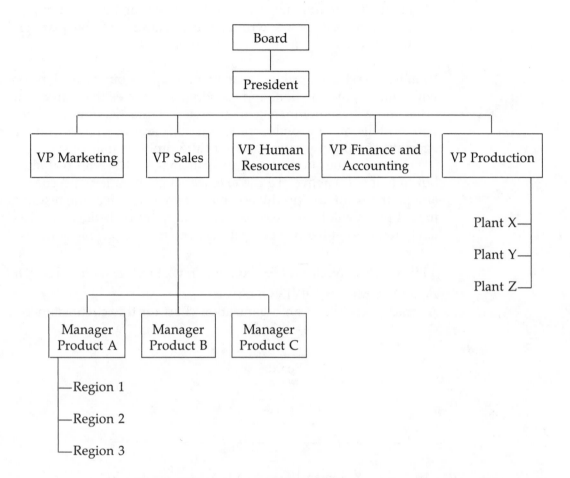

In this scenario our process works very well, provided there is open communication of **Level 1** and **Level 3** from top management to the product managers and plant managers, *and* between the product managers and plant managers. Also, it will probably be necessary for the product managers to be actively involved in **Level 2** relative to their specific product concerns.

Unfortunately, it is sometimes the case that organizations such as this require business plans from the product managers without having first created **Levels 1, 2,** or **3.** Or they have created these without communicating them to these managers even if the information is requested by the managers.

When business plans are required from parts of the organization in this manner, only two real possibilities exist:

1. The person may attempt to write a plan without regard for the rest of the company. In this case, the manager typically starts the planning process at **Level 4** and creates short-term plans that are mostly budgets.

2. The person may decide that planning within such a context is not likely to be fruitful. Therefore, one will attempt to create what one believes **Levels 1, 2,** and **3** are or would be if senior management did them. These are then placed into the plan with a notation that they are the foundation for the plan. If the assumed philosophy, mission, and/or objectives are wrong, the remainder of the plan probably won't suit senior management either.

If, in this case, each product manager submits a business plan complete with philosophy, mission, and corporate objectives that agree with each other and with senior management's view, fantastic! If they submit plans with widely varying philosophy, mission, and objectives, senior management should at least be aware of the problem that exists.

However, the product and plant managers have no real alternative but to follow (2) above. To the extent that cooperation and coordination among the plant and production managers is possible, the resultant submitted plans will be more consistent and more realistic, as well as more likely to be accepted by senior management.

THE LARGE MULTIPLE-PRODUCT BUSINESS WITH LARGELY AUTONOMOUS DIVISIONS

A typical example of an organization chart for this circumstance is:

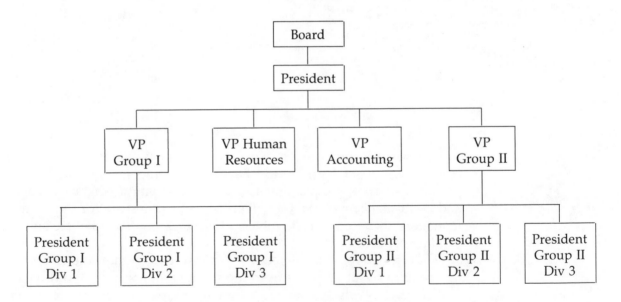

In instances such as this the case may be:

1. The two groups are so diverse that any plan that covers both must be very general and is usually financial in nature. Therefore, at the corporate level the plan consists primarily of a broad mission and philosophy, and financial objectives for each group. Then, each group takes this information into consideration when formulating its own plans. The group vice-presidents and the division presidents constitute

senior management under our planning process and a plan using **Level 1** through **Level 6** is formulated for each group.

2. Not only are the groups diverse, but the divisions are also diverse. For the most part, the corporate level is a service organization and a banker. Each division is basically a company unto itself. In such cases, each division will create a complete and independent plan. Probably, the corporate plan will either roll up the divisional plans or will largely be an encompassing budget for all of the functions.

THE PROJECT OR VENTURE WITHIN AN EXISTING BUSINESS

Project planning is very similar to business planning in most respects. It is particularly close to business planning in the start-up business case. However, there are some differences:

1. This situation does not require the development of **Level 1** (Philosophy and Mission). The project should be working within the already established (written or not) company philosophy. Often, the term *mission statement* will be used as the reported *reason for being* of the proposed idea. That is appropriate.

2. **Level 2** (Strategic Plan), on a limited and directed scope basis, is appropriate for new products or new businesses. For some types of project plans (new facilities, equipment changeovers, product line extensions, territory expansions, etc.) it may not be necessary at all.

3. Of course, the project or venture should be consistent with **Level 3** (Corporate Objectives), but no work at this level is necessary.

4. Primarily, this type of plan begins with **Level 4** (Planning Unit Goals). Such plans are usually operational in nature and quite detailed. **Level 5** (Tactics and Projections) normally will complete the planning needed for this scenario.

THE NOT-FOR-PROFIT ENTITY

While there are accounting differences between for-profit and not-for-profit entities, in many other respects they are quite alike. Perhaps the other single most striking difference is the use of volunteer rather than paid help that creates not only an operational but also a planning distinction.

In the not-for-profit situation, it is very important to involve as many people as possible in the planning process. In particular, it is important that the planning process include key volunteers and not just paid staff. Certainly there are some not-for-profit entities that are large enough to function with mostly paid staff. In these cases, planning usually works as in the small, ongoing, single-product case with the additional involvement of the Board of Directors at **Level 1** and **Level 3**.

For most not-for-profits, clearly establishing philosophy, mission, and objectives is a key to attracting and keeping volunteers and funding. The importance of having as many involved volunteers as possible cannot be stressed too much.

Another often overlooked area in not-for-profit planning is Strategic (competitive) Planning. The not-for-profit entity often has competition from for-profit as well as other not-for-profit entities in the service it provides for customers/clients. It also has competition for the funding it seeks. Therefore, competitive analysis is urgent.

Level 4 and **Level 5** work much the same in not-for-profit as in for-profit. The biggest difference has to do with getting things done through volunteers and the special problems that consequently arise.

Level 6, getting it on paper, is important for the not-for-profit. A thoughtful, well-documented plan can be useful for attracting funds and volunteers.

Summary

Overall, the circumstances of business plan development can be categorized into three groups:

1. Plans developed to tell those who do not have direct control over you, what you intend to do—possibly with help from them (bankers, venture capitalists, parent companies, foundations, etc.)

2. Plans developed for the purpose of helping you determine what you want to do and to justify the feasibility of it

3. Plans developed as an operating guideline and measurement tool for everyone connected with the organization

The process outlined herein, modified accordingly, can be effectively implemented in all of these circumstances.

FREQUENTLY ASKED QUESTIONS (WITH ANSWERS) ABOUT BUSINESS PLANNING

1. When the Philosophy, Mission, and (perhaps even) Objectives of Senior Management are either not developed or not communicated downward, what should middle managers do?

   Unfortunately, this is not uncommon. While this is discussed in the section Using This Process, *it bears some additional consideration. Some things a middle manager can do are:*

   a. Request an example plan to use for format

   b. Request a format outline that the person requesting the plan would like to have

   c. Request a copy of the philosophy, mission, and objectives into which the plan is supposed to fit (this gives notice of your knowledge of the need for these)

d. Use the process outlined in this book and create the whole plan, labeling the portions which should be given you by senior management as assumptions key to the plan

e. Start at **Level 4** of the process described in this book and ignore the rest

2. Is it possible to do successful planning in the situation described above?

Yes, it is possible but it isn't very probable. Because there is no coordination across the various planners (department heads, product managers, etc.), the planning becomes management by objection. *Everyone does what she/he wants to do until, and unless, someone objects.*

Even successful plans drawn up in this scenario are usually short-ranged and narrowly focused. They are typically plans for improving operational efficiency rather than plans for increasing the scope of the business.

3. If middle managers cannot get a philosophy, mission, and/or objectives from senior management, can they start at **Level 3** and call it a business plan?

In our opinion, the results here are not really a business plan. That is not to say that they are not valuable. They don't really cover the whole business, but the results may satisfy senior management.

4. Isn't it feasible that each department/division of a company could have its own business plan in addition to the company plan?

Yes! In fact they may have such plans even when there is no company plan. Please see Using This Process *for more discussion.*

5. What happens when the planning begins at the bottom or middle of the organization?

In our opinion, this usually means that senior management is failing to exercise the leadership it should. However, if there is time and if there is dialogue, this process can still work. It takes longer and costs more but it can work.

*Usually, senior management is saying, "Tell us what you can do (or what you want to do) and we'll tell you what we will let you do." If senior management will take the submitted plans (the results of **Levels 4** and **5**) and will carefully analyze, consolidate, and condense them as input into their **Level 1** through **Level 3** responsibilities, and will then communicate back, the process can be very successful.*

Unfortunately, too often senior management doesn't synthesize the plans; they simply bind them together. When that is the case you have operational plans for departments/divisions but not a plan for the business.

6. Are there other planning models and what do you do with them?

Obviously, there are many other models in use. Perhaps the most common model is the budget first model. *In this model, planners are asked to prepare and submit a budget. The emphasis is mostly on revenue (for profit center types) or costs (for cost center or service types). Then, if anything else is called for, a plan for meeting the budget is requested.*

Sometimes a quota model *is used. A manager is given a number (sales, costs, volume) and is then told to prepare a plan to achieve this.*

When these, or other similar models, are used, we suggest you learn the game and play by the rules. Generally the plans are not worth much, but no one pays attention to them anyway.

7. My company is doing pretty well and we have never had a business plan. How do I convince senior management that we need one?

Truthfully, you probably won't convince management. In such cases, the most likely thing to create awareness of need is disaster, and you don't want that. But, without a plan, disaster is what you'll eventually get.

Meanwhile, you can start project planning and show how well it works. You can clip articles or give books that discuss successful companies and how they plan. You can recommend courses or conferences on planning to your managers.

But don't get too excited. It often takes disaster to start the process.

8. Is the business planning process for a nonrevenue generating division or department (Human Resources) the same as for a revenue generator?

Essentially, yes, it should be. If there are corporate objectives that are well stated, these objectives will include goals and action items for most, if not all, divisions/departments. While the nature of the goals for revenue and non-revenue divisions/departments will differ, the process of constructing them need not.

In the situation where a non-revenue division/department is required to construct a separate business plan (without sufficient direction from or consultation with senior management) the situation changes somewhat. Management of such a division/department will need to delineate clearly its reason for being in the company and will need to create the most quantifiable, measurable objectives and goals possible.

It is often the case that business plans in this scenario are being used to justify decreasing or eliminating a division/department. Well-stated, measurable objectives and goals which show the cost-benefit relationships of the division/ department may help stabilize or even improve the position of such a division/ department. (See Using This Process.*)*

Particular attention should be paid to creating a strong mission statement that fully integrates the division/department into overall operations. And, communication with revenue generating divisions/departments to assure their satisfaction with the product, and their mention of it in their plans, is also helpful.

9. We have never and still don't have time to plan. Things change too quickly and a plan would be obsolete before it could be implemented. Don't you agree that this negates any need for a plan?

   Frankly, rather than being a reason for not planning, this situation simply says that someone doesn't know how to plan or what a plan is intended to accomplish.

   A business plan that is created three to six months before the start of the year, which is exactly on target in all its estimates and in all its methods of action by year end is either:

   a. Being forced as a hard and fast rule rather than a guideline, or

   b. For a highly unusual situation

   Business plans are first and foremost a means of considering, in advance, as many probabilities as possible, selecting from among them the ones you want to make happen, and determining the means for doing so. These are always based upon assumptions. When and as the assumptions change, the plans based upon them also change. But if the planning process was well done, such alternatives have already been considered so they do not come as a surprise.

   It is true that a plan may become obsolete. Planning (the process) will never become so. Planning may be useless if:

   1. Senior management refuses to participate and give leadership

   2. Senior management limits discussion and doesn't foster creative, innovative thinking

   3. Middle management, and below, are not trained and educated in how to plan and how to manage by plan

On the following page is a set of terms which we have adopted for use in this book. The terms are certainly not universally used. If your organization is accustomed to using a different set of terms, don't be dismayed. Simply substitute your terminology for that which is included here. However, it is critical that you use a consistent set of terms and that everyone in the organization understands the terms and uses them in the same way.

You may wish to distribute the next page to all who participate in the plan.

BUSINESS PLANNING TERMS

Philosophy: The set of basic beliefs which establishes the parameters for the business and its personnel. It is a statement of what we do and what we don't do.

- Why are we in business?
- How do we do business?
- What do we do and not do as a business?

Mission: The primary focus of the business which answers the question,

- What business are we in?

Status: An assessment of the present position which answers the question,

- Where are we?

Strategy: A method or course of action for dealing with competitors. It can be either proactive or reactive.

- Who else is in this business?
- How do we relate to them?

Objective: An aim or end of an action; results to be accomplished. For the *business as a whole* it answers the question,

- Where does the business want to go?

Goal: A point toward which a planning unit strives; a step toward accomplishing an objective. For the *planning unit* it answers the question,

- Where does the planning unit want to go?

Tactic: Methods of using resources to reach goals. It helps to answer the question,

- How do we get there?

Projection: A quantitative estimate of the results expected from using various tactics, particularly those we expect to employ.

- What will it look like when we do get there?

THE DOCUMENT

It is sometimes said that the major value to be gained from a business plan is not in the plan at all. Rather, 70 percent or more of the value comes from the *process* of planning. You will notice that the definition of business planning emphasizes the nature of the process. You'll also note that a process is typically ongoing and continuous. While a business planning process should, in fact, eventually lead to a business plan, it does not stop at the point at which a plan is finished. The dynamics of the business environment ensure that a plan, once completed, will immediately start becoming obsolete. Therefore, it is essential to be prepared to revise the plan accordingly as new information is gathered.

While it is true that much of the value of planning lies in the process rather than in the product, it is extremely important that the process should eventually lead to a product. The business plan is a major medium by which the plans of the organization are communicated both to the people within the organization as well as people without the organization. It ensures that the memories of those who were involved in the planning process stay consistent and it provides the opportunity for those planners to let others know what they intend to accomplish and how.

Sometimes a document is constructed and labeled a business plan. However, such documents are often, at best, budgets and not plans. You will note that a good business plan includes strategic or competitive planning, operational or efficiency planning, as well as financial planning. It should be made perfectly clear that the budget is the final phase of planning. The budget should come out of the plan rather than being an input to or a constraint on the plan.

Business Planning

Provides management with a realistic and systematic process:

1. To evaluate the present and desired status of the company
2. To evaluate the present and expected status of the competition
3. To identify assumptions on which to operate
4. To reconcile conflicting views
5. To arrive at agreed-upon
   a. Strategies
   b. Objectives
   c. Goals
   d. Tactics
   e. Projections

A Business Plan

1. Is the written product of the business planning process
2. Integrates strategic, operational, and financial (budgeting) planning.

Comparison of Process Orientation and Product Orientation

Planning for Business	Business Plan
Having in mind; arranging the parts of; projecting the realization of	A proposed method of action or procedure
Specific to the planner	Written and available to all potential users
Often based on guesstimates rather than supported data	Carefully developed schedules to support projections
Not available as goal setting and motivating tool for others in organization	Goals and objectives for components and responsible individuals
Often focuses on areas of major interest to planner	Each area of organization integrated into plan
Not useful to outsiders	Effective for external financing and other needs
Process Only	**Process Leading to Product**

Let's recall the events of May 25, 1961. President John F. Kennedy gave a speech which began a process illustrating the *elements of a good plan*. His statement (paraphased): "I believe this nation should commit itself to achieve the goal, before this decade is out, of landing a man on the moon and returning him safely to Earth." And we did! From the speech and from the space program that followed we saw the elements fulfilled.

Elements of a Good Plan

Vision: "*A man on the moon . . .*" Our view of this today is quite different than it was pre-1961. Now it seems obvious. Children of the 1970s and 1980s take space travel for granted. But it was quite visionary at the time. Also note that it was probably not originally President Kennedy's vision. Most likely others much lower in government brought the vision to the President. His major contribution was not *creating* the vision but rather *communicating* the vision.

Commitment: "*And returning him safely . . .* " The President committed to those who would lay their lives on the line that every effort would be made to protect them. The astronauts needed to know that. They could then concentrate their attention on their tasks. The commitment was expensive.

Extra tests were performed and numerous precautions were taken. But it helped get the job done.

Timelines: *"Before this decade is out . . . "* Overall, this was an unusual political statement. To box oneself into a specific completion time is generally not something a politician wants to do.

Phasing: *We had Mercury, Gemini, and Apollo.* When the effort to put a man on the moon began, the scientists and engineers did not immediately put people into capsules and begin launching them. Each step had a specific objective and the results of each phase were additive.

Contingencies: *Whatever can go wrong, will, and at the worst time.* With respect for those whose lives have been lost in the space program, throughout the lunar landing era the record was remarkably free of life-taking accidents. Considering the risks involved, the program performed beautifully. That was due largely to the painstaking contingency planning that tried (1) to imagine every possible problem, and (2) to create a plan first for preventing it and second for dealing with it if it happened.

Reporting: *"One small step for man, one giant step for mankind."* As Neil A. Armstrong came down the ladder from the lunar module Eagle at 4:18 p.m. EDT on July 20, 1969, he made the above statement. This historic event, which included Edwin E. Aldrin, Jr. and Michael Collins as the other astronauts, is burned into the memories of all who observed it. And the camera that beamed those pictures back to Earth was not haphazardly placed. It was carefully staged to show this event, the objective of the program. Reporting should be keyed to the momentous events of the plan, not to the trivia.

Change: The plans that can and do change are the ones which last. One of the reasons for stating the assumptions on which a plan is based is that we can, from time to time, review those assumptions and determine whether or not a change of plan is needed. One of the best examples of a plan which includes a change process is the Constitution of the United States. While the United States is considered a young country it certainly has an old Constitution. Perhaps this Constitution has survived for 200 years because it contains the method by which it can be changed or amended. Similarly, business plans should contain within them the method by which they can be changed. This usually includes a quarterly review of assumptions and results, a determination of the changes which need to be made, and a listing of the changes which have been made.

It may be valuable to you as you go through the planning process to use the Elements page, such as the one following, to be certain that all of these elements are present.

After you have completed the process, but before you actually begin to write the plan document, fill out the Elements page in the appendix. Discuss it with the management team to be sure that your plan is what the team intends it to be.

You may choose to have each member of the **Level 1** team complete an Elements sheet independently and then compare and consolidate them. This should assure that all are operating on the same planning wavelength.

ELEMENTS*

Vision: _____

_____

Commitment: _____

_____

Timelines: _____

_____

Phasing: _____

_____

Contingencies: _____

_____

Reporting: _____

_____

Change: _____

_____

The following pages contain an outline for a general business plan. Obviously, plans constructed for special purposes may need emphasis or sections not shown here. Some industries may have elements of the business (research and development) that are important enough to warrant a section of the business plan.

The planning process should lead to a planning product. It is always better to have an understanding of the product being made before starting the process to make it.

* This form is also in the appendix.

You should give an outline of the plan to all the plan's contributors at the very beginning of the process. Then, they will all be working toward a common result.

BUSINESS PLAN OUTLINE*

1. Cover Sheet
    a. Company name and/or logo
    b. Business plan and year
    c. Names (perhaps with phone numbers)

2. Sign-up Page

3. Executive Summary
    a. Two pages
    b. What's in it for the reader?
    c. How many different readers?

4. Table of Contents
    a. Make it detailed enough to be useful
    b. Should be about one heading per page of text

5. Major Assumptions
    a. Economy
    b. Suppliers
    c. Consumers
    d. Competition

6. History Section
    a. Two pages maximum
    b. Focus on relationship to plans
    c. Major events

7. Philosophy

8. Definition of the Business
    a. Usually less than one page
    b. What business(es) are we in?
    c. What is the glue holding us together?

9. Definition of the Market
    a. Consider buyers and sellers
    b. Can use strategic factors analysis to help describe sellers (competitive analysis)
    c. Describe buyers demographically, psychographically, and by distribution channel

* This form is discussed further in the section on **Level 6** and appears in the appendix.

10. Description of Products or Services
    a. Most emphasis on new ones
    b. Advertising information sometimes helpful
    c. No catalogs

11. Management Structure
    a. Show that you have the right people
    b. Quarter-page résumés
    c. Relate résumés to goals

12. Strategies, Objectives, Goals, and Tactics
    a. Longest section of the plan
    b. Strategies lead to objectives
    c. Don't forget operational objectives
    d. Objectives lead to goals
    e. Format to reduce writing and ease reading

13. Financial Data
    a. This is the plan translated to dollars
    b. Budgets
       —Capital items
       —Cash flow
       —Revenue and expense
    c. Cost-volume-profit analysis

14. Appendices
    a. Supporting detail
    b. Making it work
    c. Not a dumping ground for superfluous pages

THE PLANNING COMMUNICATIONS PROCESS

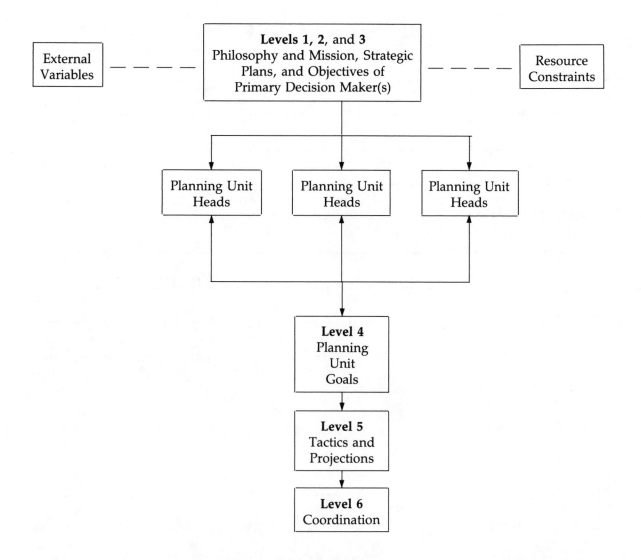

The planning process occurs in a series of meetings. We have divided these meetings into six levels. Each level may require several meetings to accomplish the essential tasks. Each meeting should add value toward the final plan.

It is important that meetings be run efficiently and effectively. Someone should be in charge and attending to detail. For meetings of more than half a day the following Facilitator's Check List will be helpful in ensuring proper tools for an efficient meeting.

Copy the Facilitator's Check List and the Meeting Hints and give them to each person who will conduct one or more of the planning meetings.

Complete the Business Plan Coordination Time Chart in the appendix using the completed one on page 22 as a guide. Give copies to all who are listed as responsible persons as a guide to the necessary times to be followed. Estimated completion times are given for each of the six levels later.

FACILITATOR'S CHECK LIST

Meeting Checklist

Facility Name _____

Address _____

Phone _____

Facility Contact Person _____

Off-hours Contact Person _____

Limo: Phone _____ Cost _____

Car Rental On-site _____

Recreation Available _____ Cost _____

Directions to Facility (if necessary)

_____

_____

Meeting Room Name or Number _____

_____ Ease of Access   _____ Walls Okay for Tape   _____ Rest Rooms Accessible

_____ Noise Level   _____ Windows Covered   _____ Out-of-Room Phone

_____ Visual Distractions _____ Chairs Comfortable   _____ Break Service Specified

                            _____ Table(s) Substantial

Dining Room Name or Number _____

_____ Size Appropriate   _____ Buffets   _____ Adequate Servers

_____ Separation from Meeting   _____ Menu Checked
        Room

Equipment

_____ Flip Charts and Stands   _____ Note Pads   _____ Markers
        (with backs)   (all necessary colors)

                                  _____ Pencils

MEETING HINTS: DOS AND DON'TS

Do

1. Be sure the meeting is necessary

2. Be sure all the appropriate people are notified in writing

3. Be sure the agenda has been prepared and circulated

4. Be sure each participant knows what she/he is supposed to bring and to do

5. Start on time and end on time

6. Keep minutes to summarize what happens

7. Identify the person in charge

8. Use an off-site facility if possible

Don't

1. Put more on the agenda than can be covered

2. Have the meeting at an inappropriate facility

3. Fail to check on the availability of needed services

4. Forget to have appropriate food service

5. Create unnecessary problems of transportation or parking

6. Allow any one participant to dominate

7. Allow any participant to be anonymous

8. Have spouses at the meeting

BUSINESS PLAN COORDINATION TIME CHART*

Task	Responsible Person(s)	Due Date*
1. Gather background data including plans, budgets, financial statements and performance evaluations for past five years (if available)	*Plan Coordinator*	*2 weeks*
2. Level 1 — *see page 29*	*Senior management*	*4 weeks*
3. Level 2 — *see page 43*	*Senior management*	*4 weeks*
4. Level 3 — *see page 53*	*Senior management*	*2 weeks*
5. Level 4 — *see page 75*	*Planning Unit manager*	*4 weeks*
6. Level 5 — *see page 95*	*Planning Unit manager*	*4 weeks*
7. Level 6 — *see page 103*	*Plan coordinator*	*4 weeks*
8. Written presentation	*as chosen* **	
9. Oral presentation	*as chosen* **	

*Indicates approximate time needed for the first plan attempt. Obviously, many factors can affect these estimates. Provide a total horizon of *not less than* four months (preferably six months).
**Depending upon to whom the presentation is made, this may be the plan coordinator, a planning unit manager or even senior management.

The six levels of meetings for building a business plan are illustrated in the following sections. Relevant forms, not completed, are duplicated in the appendix for your use.

These sheets constitute *a plan for the plan*. When properly and fully completed they will provide a road map for the development of the plan.

Study the illustrative pages for understanding. Then, consider how you would complete these pages for your own plan.

The example pages will be repeated later for emphasis and continuity of process. They are presented here, all together, to give you a quick feel for the process in total.

The blank forms in the appendix are for your own planning process.

* A blank copy of this chart is in the appendix.

LEVEL 1

Philosophy and Mission

Who: This is the job of the senior management team. The CEO, COO, CFO (all of whom may be the same person) and his/her direct reports (at least) should be involved.

What: A clear, concise statement of the philosophy and the mission of the business. This should be done in not more than four pages. The mission statement should be one concise paragraph, although there may be some explanation regarding that paragraph.

          This is the foundation not only of the plan but also of the very business. Don't skimp here. Don't underestimate the value of this. Give it time and careful attention.

When: Since this is the foundation it must be done first. We suggest that you begin work on this as much as six months before you expect to have a completed plan in place. Do this first even if you are time constrained and must complete the plan in a shorter period.

Where: We recommend that the senior management team do this work in an off-site environment. Get away from the offices. Go to a hotel, a resort, or someone's private retreat. Better still, go to a conference center whose staff is trained to meet your needs.

How Long: This varies considerably depending upon how much advance work has been done, whether a philosophy and mission have been written before, and whether professional facilitators are involved. However, you should expect *not less than two days* strictly devoted to this. Use the remainder of the four weeks discussed earlier to review, disseminate, and discuss the results.

LEVEL 2

Strategic Plan

Who: The same people from **Level 1** must be involved. You may also wish to bring in staff people (if you have them) with special interest in this area. And you may want to include the top level operations and product people if they were not part of **Level 1**.

What: As you will see more clearly later, the term *strategic planning* means the development of a plan for understanding and dealing with competitors. While this does have long-range implications, it is not synonymous with the commonly used term, long-range planning.

Specifically, we are looking for those factors of competition which will create advantages for us in the marketplace. In order for this to occur, two things must be so: (1) The factor must be one of importance to the customer or client, and (2) It must be one on which we can clearly (and positively) differentiate ourselves from our competition.

When: As soon as possible after the completion of **Level 1**.

Where: The initial data gathering can be done from the office environment. However, when the decision-making time comes we prefer to do this in an environment as described in **Level 1**. The off-site setting lends importance and urgency to the discussions.

How Long: Assuming proper groundwork has been done (which may take several weeks), and appropriate competitive information is available, this is a two to three day session. The decisions made here affect every aspect of the business and should be given due diligence in the deliberations.

LEVEL 3

Corporate Objectives

Who: Although this sounds repetitive, the fact is that the same people from **Level 1** should also be responsible here.

What: The U.S. Marine Corps advertises for *a few good men*. We believe you need *a few good objectives*. How many? There are no hard and fast rules but the number four seems reasonable. Often, two objectives are expressed in financial statement terms (e.g., profitability, return on assets, return on sales, gross margin, cost reduction, net worth, return on stockholders' equity). One is employee oriented (training, benefits, work environment, etc.); the other is project oriented (new plan, new territory, new product, etc.)

However many objectives you choose to state, each should be:

• Specific	• Clear	• Positive
• Measurable	• Concise	• Reasonable
• Actionable	• Consistent	• Inclusive
• Relevant	• Motivating	• Timebound

When: You may be able to add this onto the **Level 2** meeting. However, we suggest that you not do that on your first attempt at building a plan. You need time to ratify **Level 1** and **Level 2** before setting your objectives. Therefore, we suggest a delay of two to four weeks following **Level 2**.

Where: If time and/or money is a problem this can be done on-site. However, we recommend going off-site if possible.

How Long: Depending upon the clarity of the Strategic Plan, this may take only one day. Plan on arriving midday and departing late the following afternoon. Again, however, while the process may culminate in one day, it will percolate over several weeks.

LEVEL 4

Planning Unit Goals

Who: Generally, those who directly report to those involved with **Level 1** will be the main focus of this level (i.e., product managers, territory managers, plant managers, division managers, etc.).

What: Each planning unit should state at least one goal in support of each corporate objective. The real burden, at **Level 3**, is to develop objectives that are truly corporate and into which every planning unit can reasonably fit. Each goal should be a component block of accomplishing the objective which it supports.

When: The first three levels should be complete and should have been disseminated to these people before they begin work on **Level 4**. We suggest a minimum period of two weeks for feedback from these people after the products of **Level 1** through **Level 3** have been given to them. Once senior management is comfortable that **Level 1** through **Level 3** are reasonably solid, work can begin on **Level 4**.

Where: Separate meetings will first be held by individual planning units to construct their own goals. These should take place on-site because of the numbers and job requirements of the people. Once the planning units have developed their goals, the planning unit managers should meet for one day in an off-site setting to present their goals to each other for discussion, revision (if necessary), and adoption.

Of course, it is important that the adopted and approved goals add up to the accomplishment of the objectives. If they do not, either the goals or the objectives must be modified to make them all align.

How Long: As indicated above, there may be several different meetings of varying lengths involved here. Total elapsed time will often be about four weeks.

LEVEL 5

Tactics and Projections

Who: The planning unit managers and their direct reports (this may go down to the first line supervisors).

What: Each adopted and approved goal should have an action plan with appropriate measurements and monitoring points for it. Since this is the *daily operational portion* of the plan, it will be detailed.

When: Work can commence on this level as soon as senior management has approved the product of **Level 4**.

Where: Because of the information needed and because of the numbers and job requirements of the people involved, these meetings will probably be held on-site.

How Long: There will likely be many short (one to three hours) meetings involved in the development of this part of the plan. Total elapsed time again may be about four weeks.

LEVEL 6

Coordination

Who: When it comes to completing the plan it is usually best to have one person designated to put it into document form. Whoever is so designated should have sufficient clout to require and obtain cooperation to get parts of the plan in as needed.

What: A written document following the outline given earlier. If possible, the basic text portion of the plan should be about 20 pages. The appendices may be as voluminous as necessary to support the plan.

When: The plan should be complete and in the hands of all responsible people 15 to 30 days before it is to become the operative document.

Where: Normally, the plan is completed (put together) in the office environment.

How Long: Finalization should not really be a large problem if the preceding steps have been well followed. Allow at least two weeks, and preferably four, to put the document together.

Now we begin to put the planning process into action. We repeat the **Level 1** form from the introduction section. You, the planning coordinator, should complete the **Level 1** page in the appendix and be certain that all affected parties have a completed copy of it.

You should also give all of these people a copy of the Business Plan Outline (pp. 17–18), the Elements page (blank), and the Business Plan Coordination Time Chart (completed by you) from the appendix. Explain to the **Level 1** participants that they should bring the Elements page to the first meeting, *completed as they see fit*.

Have several blank copies of the Elements page at the first meeting to use in drawing a consensus.

PHILOSOPHY AND MISSION

Who: This is the job of the senior management team. The CEO, COO, CFO (all of whom may be the same person) and his/her direct reports (at least) should be involved.

What: A clear, concise statement of the philosophy and the mission of the business. This should be done in not more than four pages. The mission statement should be one concise paragraph, although there may be some explanation regarding that paragraph.

This is the foundation not only of the plan but also of the very business. Don't skimp here. Don't underestimate the value of this. Give it time and careful attention.

When: Since this is the foundation it must be done first. We suggest that you begin work on this as much as *six months* before you expect to have a completed plan in place. Do this first even if you are time constrained and must complete the plan in a shorter period.

Where: We recommend that the senior management team do this work in an off-site environment. Get away from the offices. Go to a hotel, a resort, or someone's private retreat. Better still, go to a conference center whose staff is trained to meet your needs.

How Long: This varies considerably depending upon how much advance work has been done, whether a philosophy and mission have been written before, and whether professional facilitators are involved. However, you should expect *not less than two days* strictly devoted to this. Use the remainder of the four weeks discussed earlier to review, disseminate, and discuss the results.

Earlier, we defined philosophy to be *the set of basic beliefs which established the parameters for the business and its personnel. It is a statement of what we do and what we don't do.*

It is usually easier to approach a statement of coherent philosophy by breaking down the elements of that philosophy into simple components. We have given statements of Business Philosophies written by companies in various lines of business. We suggest that you review these but withhold them from distribution to participants in your planning process until after they have attempted statements on their own. Following that is a Philosophy form. You will note that there are blanks at the bottom indicating that this is not intended to be an exhaustive list.

It is important that the statements written by your organization are meaningful to you. If the participants view these examples too early they may choose to adopt them without giving due consideration to their content and meaning. A blank form for your use is in the appendix.

Following is an example and in the appendix is a blank copy of **Level 1** Planning Process Assumptions. Each participant should get a copy of the blank form. It is used to document assumptions made throughout the process. These accumulated sheets are very useful for contingency planning purposes.

PLANNING PROCESS ASSUMPTIONS

Since the planning process deals with creating outcomes by future actions, it is essential and necessary to make assumptions about events and circumstances outside the planners' control. These assumptions are critical to the plan.

Please complete this sheet for each key assumption you make.

Assumption	Probability of Assumption Being Violated	Impact if Assumption Violated
1. Company will not be taken over and will continue with essentially present management.	1. Low	1. Operating philosophies and policies will change.
2. Raw materials will remain available at about current level.	2. Low	2. Alternate inputs are available that will not change product from customer view.

BUSINESS PHILOSOPHIES

General Examples

Integrity: We believe integrity is the cornerstone of all our business relationships; therefore, we will expect all of our employees to be honest and forthright with our customers, our vendors, and with all others whom they may contact in the name of the business.

Management: We believe management is the art of leading people to accomplish stated objectives; therefore, leadership qualities and demonstrated ability to accomplish objectives will be primary criteria by which we select and evaluate managers.

Planning: We believe planning is the art of preparing for change; therefore, we will use planning as a management tool to keep us prepared for those changes that must come.

Customers: We believe that nothing happens until you make a sale, and sales are only made to customers; therefore, we will place the satisfaction of our customers above every other business consideration.

Employees: We believe well-trained, highly motivated employees are the most important means of serving our customers; therefore, we will select, train, and reward employees who place customer satisfaction first.

Profit: Our ability to properly service our customers depends on long-term profitability; therefore, we will manage our business to create a responsible return on assets.

Growth: We believe growth is a logical consequence for a well-managed company; therefore, we will evaluate management on the profitable, orderly, controlled growth the company sustains.

Community: We believe a profitable, growing business should, from its abundance, invest in the community that sustains it; therefore, we will individually and corporately invest in selected philanthropic activities of our community.

We suggest that you distribute copies of the blank Philosophy page in the appendix and the Suggestions page following it to all participants of your **Level 1** planning meeting. We also suggest that you choose four or five example statements that best fit your company, and distribute them to the participants in order that they might better understand the nature of the statements expected.

For your information, a copy of the Philosophy page and Suggestions for Use follow.

PHILOSOPHY

Rank

_____ Profits

_____ Customers

_____ Employees

_____ Management

_____ Community

_____ Integrity

_____ Growth

_____ Planning

_____ _____

_____ _____

SUGGESTIONS FOR USE

Philosophy

1. The list of topics may not be complete. Add different topics if appropriate.

2. Rank the topics in order of their importance to the company. Compare your rankings with others and discuss the differences.

3. Write a short statement about each topic. It might follow the form: *"We believe . . . ; therefore, ..."* It usually helps later in the planning process to have included the *therefore*, since it can provide something to act upon.

4. If you print the statements for distribution, consider them by the ranks assigned in suggestion 2.

An objective review of the company is a valuable, even essential first step. In order to help you accomplish that first step we have devised three forms which are contained in the appendix: *What Do We Do Best?*, *What Need Do We Meet?*, and *Whose Need Do We Meet?* We suggest that you use these three pages in your **Level 1** planning meeting to get people thinking objectively about the company. In order to facilitate this we will provide you with examples for these three pages.

The airplane goes along with the question, *What do we do best*? If you were to ask the participants the question, "What do airlines do best?" you would expect answers such as, "Fly people," "Fly cargo," "Take people from place to place," or "Lose luggage."

While all of the above may be true, none of them is a complete enough story. What airlines actually do is to move people and cargo from airport to airport. The interesting question is, "How many people really want to go from airport to airport?" Furthermore, how many people really want to send cargo from airport to airport?

This last question was asked by Fred Smith, the man who started Federal Express. The answer that he came up with was, "No one." That cargo had to be handled by a multiplicity of people was in fact a problem.

Services such as Eastern Airlines' Sprint were quick, but expensive and inconvenient. In order to get delivery of small parcels great distances and in short periods of time, it was often necessary to carry the parcels to an airport, consign them to an airline, and find someone on the receiving end to go to the airport and pick them up. Same-day service was available but the inconvenience and cost were limiting factors.

Recognizing a potential market, Federal Express decided to pick up at the customers' site and deliver to the customers' destination. This amounted to a recognition that what the airline did best was not necessarily what the customer most wanted. When the customers' desires were recognized, the demand for the service increased dramatically.

Having decided *what we do best*, you must also decide if that meets the desires and needs of the consumer. Have the participants write down what they think your company does best. Discuss the answers and come to a consensus on the priority of the answers.

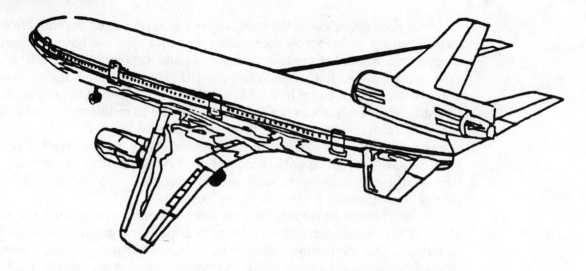

What Do We Do Best?

Federal Express: Airlines move people and things from airport to airport. Federal Express moves packages from where they are to where you want them.

The following picture shows an old-style window shade. You have seen this type. They are made out of paper or vinyl on a recoil spring at the top. When you pull them down you hope they will stay at approximately the level that you want. In his best-selling book *Megatrends*, John Naisbitt describes a company which in 1904 was manufacturing window shades. The company employed a consultant by the name of Mary Parker Follet to assist them. She asked the question, "What do you do?" and the response was, of course, "We make window shades." But her real question was, "Why do people buy window shades?"

You may want to ask participants, "Why do people buy window shades?" Expect answers such as, "To keep out the sun," "To keep out heat," "Privacy," "Security," or "Decorations."

Let's assume that this company determined that it was in the business of meeting the customers' need for light control, which was Ms. Follet's answer. Ask your participants to name products that are now available to meet this need and you will probably get a list that includes window shades, several varieties of blinds, awnings, tinting, electrical switches, light fixtures, and sunglasses.

Note the difference between the means (window shades) and the end (light control). Try to get the participants to determine what need(s) your company is in business to meet.

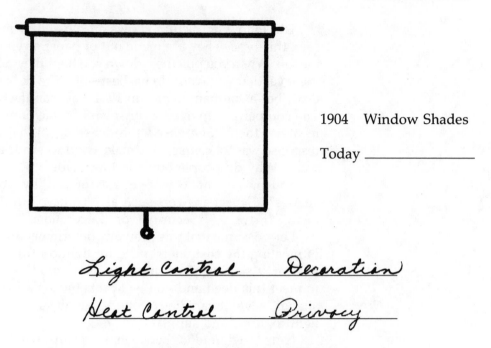

1904   Window Shades

Today _____

Light Control   Decoration

Heat Control   Privacy

What Need Do We Meet?

The end was light control. The means was window shades. It is important to understand customer needs from the ends, not only the means point of view.

In a small Florida panhandle beach community there is an amusement park. Such places are very fixed-cost oriented. Therefore, the owner wanted to get more customers into the park because each additional customer's entrance fee was mostly contribution margin going to meet fixed costs and to make a profit.

The park was surrounded by a wall and had a single entrance where the fixed price for all amusements was paid. The owner went into the park and observed the customers. Most were 8 to 15 years old. There was an even gender mix. From talking with many of them he guessed the numbers to be about 60 percent local and 40 percent tourist, and he noticed they seemed to like the wilder, more exciting rides best.

With this information in mind he decided on an advertising campaign. He chose a radio station that seemed to have the right audience. He gave a message telling listeners that they could meet their friends and have an exciting time there. He realized he needed exposure so he ran the ads several weeks. And he found no change in his business.

One afternoon as he returned to his park he happened to notice what was taking place out front. Mostly mature female drivers were delivering kids to the entranceway, waiting until they were in the park, and then driving away.

He quickly concluded that the kids in the park weren't really the customers. Mothers were the customers, it was their needs he was meeting; his park was really a baby-sitting service.

With this new revelation he changed his advertising message and the station. He found the station many mothers listened to and he determined what was important to them (safety and price). And his business improved dramatically.

Have your participants determine whose needs the company and its products/services really meet. Don't rest with superficial, easy answers. Probe into this as deeply as possible.

Whose Need Do We Meet?

In the Florida panhandle amusement park example, the owner realized that *mothers*, not *kids*, had the *need*. Who purchases, or the most visible customer, may not be the real buying influence.

Having gone through the three stories, the participants have considered three important questions individually. Now it is time to put these all together. The form illustrated on the next page is duplicated in the appendix. Use this form to come to a consensus on all of the four questions listed.

WHAT BUSINESS ARE WE IN?

1. What Do We Do Best?

   We move people and things from airport to airport.

2. What Need Do We Meet?

   People's desire to get things moved quickly.

3. Whose Need Do We Meet?

   Business correspondence.

4. What Business Are We in?

   We are in the business of rapidly moving business correspondence from airport to airport.

SUGGESTIONS FOR USE

WHAT BUSINESS ARE WE IN?

1. Answer question 1, considering both:

   a. What do we do better than anything else we do?

      and

   b. What do we do better than anyone else who does it?

2. Answer question 2, considering needs at a basic level and not a need for product or service.

3. Answer question 3, considering not just with whom you may come into contact, but also:

   a. Who really derives the benefits or has needs met?

      and

   b. Who actually pays and why are they willing to pay?

4. Answer question 4 by combining the answers to the first three questions. It may be possible to do this in one sentence. This answer may constitute your mission statement.

5. If your company is actually in several businesses, it is best to write a mission statement for each and add a statement describing the so-called glue which holds them together.

6. You may wish to add to the mission statement a description of the path the business may follow while growing. Growth could be along present lines, or it could require considerable change.

2

You, the planning coordinator, should complete the **Level 2** Strategic Plan and be certain that all affected persons have a copy of it. Your blank form is in the appendix.

Also, you will want to distribute copies of the **Level 2** "Planning Process Assumption" page from the appendix.

STRATEGIC PLAN

Who: The people from the **Level 1** meeting must be involved. You may also wish to bring in staff people (if you have them) with special interest in this area. And you may want to include the top level operations and product people if they were not part of **Level 1**.

What: As you will see more clearly later, the term *strategic planning* means the development of a plan for understanding and dealing with competitors. While this does have long-range implications, it is not synonymous with the commonly used term *long-range planning*.

Specifically, we are looking for those factors of competition which will create advantages for us in the marketplace. In order for this to occur, two things must be so: (1) The factor must be one of importance to the customer or client, and (2) it must be one on which we can clearly (and positively) differentiate ourselves from our competition.

When: As soon as possible after the completion of **Level 1**.

Where: The initial data gathering can be done from the office environment. However, when the decision-making time comes we prefer to do this in an environment as described in **Level 1**. The off-site setting lends importance and urgency to the discussions.

How Long: Assuming proper groundwork has been done (which may take several weeks), and appropriate competitive information is available, this is a two- to three-day session. The decisions made here affect every aspect of the business and should be given due diligence in the deliberations.

The process of formulating a strategic plan is difficult mostly because it requires a comprehensive look at all of the factors that impact the business. The strictly operational plan focuses itself internally and is, therefore, somewhat easier to make. In his excellent book *The Mind of the Strategist: The Art of Japanese Business* (McGraw-Hill, Inc., 1982), Kenichi Ohmae provides a framework for looking at the business environment. We have adapted some of Mr. Ohmae's concepts to fit the formats that follow.

As is seen on the following page, the business strategy requires a careful look not only at the company but also at the customers and the competitors. We have divided each of the three large components into three subcomponents.

When considering the customers it is necessary to think of the demographics (the customer's age, income, education, race, gender, etc.) and to get as accurate a picture on all pertinent factors as possible. It is also necessary to attempt to understand the psychographics (why the customer is a customer, why he/she buys, what his/her hot button is, what the buying motive is), and the channels to get to the customer (where the customer buys). This information is available from many sources—surveys, observations, warranty cards, and so on.

Without an understanding of the customer, any attempt at planning will be minimally successful. And any attempt at understanding competitors will be useless. By definition, a competitor is one who is vying for the same prize you are trying to win. And in business the prize is the customer.

With knowledge of who the customer is (or should be), the planning can look at the competitors. The subcomponents of the competition are listed as costs, volume, and function.

How much business (volume) is the competitor doing? Is this business that you could have or is it in targeted niches that are really not suited to your company? What advantages (or disadvantages) accrue because of this volume? What are the competitors' costs of doing business? Do they have manufacturing advantages or distribution advantages?

Describing the function of the competitors' products or services is another way of answering the question, "What need does this meet?" Here the primary question is not "How does the product function?," but rather, "What does it do for the user?"

The strategic planning must also reflect on the limitations of the company. What are our people capable of accomplishing? Are we hindered by the people we have? What people do we need? Do we have the things (assets, capital equipment) necessary for the business we're in? What things must we have to accomplish our objectives? And where will the money come from?

THE THREE Cs OF BUSINESS STRATEGY

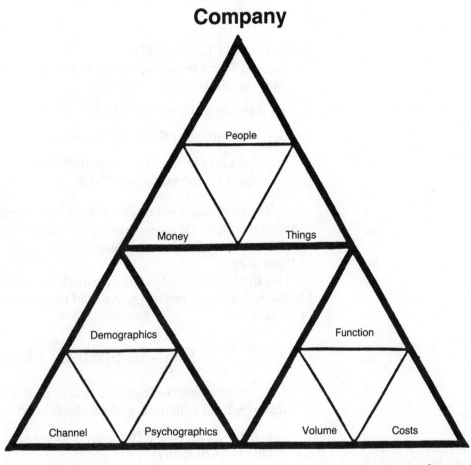

As a structural device, the equilateral triangle gains its strength from its balance. The legs are of equal length and the angles are also equal. Similarly, the balanced strategy gains its strength from not neglecting any of its three primary components: Company, Customers, Competitors. As shown above, we can use the same approach to strike a balance among the various parts of each of these components.

STRATEGY
Is the formulation of a coordinated course of actions to gain superiority over competitors.

STRATEGIC PLANNING
1. Should begin breaking the elements of the competitive environment into the simple components

2. Find those components which

   a. Are critical to the customer/client

   b. Are areas where the company has or can obtain superiority based upon the resources available

As the plan coordinator, you will probably need to lead the participants through the Strategic (competitive) Planning exercise. Below are six steps for this process. We have included some forms to help you with some of these steps.

Use the blank forms in the appendix as you find them helpful to you. On the following pages are some brief examples of what may go on some of these forms.

Steps in Strategic Planning

1. Describe the way the industry functions from raw materials suppliers through final consumers of products/services.

2. Complete the SWOT (Strengths, Weaknesses, Opportunities, Threats) Analysis. (Company)

3. Complete the Strategic Factors Analysis. (Competitors)

4. Complete the Thirty Questions Sheet. (Customers)

5. Anticipate movement and changes by competitors and customers.

6. Create a plan of action.

SWOT ANALYSIS

Strengths	Weaknesses
1. Low fixed costs make us very price competitive.	1. Lack of depth of

Opportunities	Threats
1. Automation of certain functions will enhance response time and capacity as well as improve quality control.	1. Regulatory authorities are considering certain rules which will significantly increase our fixed costs while not affecting our competitors.

STRATEGIC FACTORS ANALYSIS

_____
Customer/Client

Product A
_____
Product/Service

Rank	4	1	N/A	2	3	5
Companies:	Price	Quality	Delivery	*Service*	*Technology*	*Distributors*
Our Company	1	2		4	4	1
Competitor A	2	3		1	2	4
Competitor B	3	1		3	1	2
Competitor C	4	4		2	3	3

(*Suggestions for Use in appendix*)

THIRTY QUESTIONS TO ASSIST WITH STRATEGIC PLANNING*

1. Who are our five major customers (or classes of customers)?
    a. *Road paving contractors*
    b. *City government*
    c. *County government*
    d. *State DOT*
    e. *Private utilities*

2. What are the common characteristics of these five?
    a. *At times, need to close one lane of a two-lane road*
    b.
    c.

3. Why do they buy our product?
    a. *Safety*
    b. *Pay back*
    c.

4. Who are three potential customers (or classes of customers) who do not currently do business with us?
    a. *Federal DOT*
    b. *Military*
    c. *Toll road operators*

5. Why don't these three do business with us?
    a. *Few two-lane roads*
    b. *Not labor sensitive*
    c. *Normally four-lane roads*

* The complete thirty-question form appears in the appendix.

When the strategic factors listed previously have been separately considered, it is time to interrelate them and formulate a course of action.

A strategy is not an end unto itself. It is a means to an end—a way (and only one of many possible alternatives sometimes) to accomplish an ultimate objective. It is possible to accomplish the same objective with many different strategies.

Strategic planning recognizes the various alternatives and begins to select from among them based upon the limiting factors previously discussed.

After you have completed the materials in this section you are ready to consolidate the process into a strategic planning product. You can accomplish this by completing the Strategic Plan of Action page.

STRATEGIC PLAN OF ACTION

With specific reference to your competitors, what do you most want to accomplish? (State the accomplishments as specific results.)

1. *Move to #1 in Quality.*
2. *Move to #3 in Service.*
3. _____

What course of action will you follow to cause these to happen?

1. a. *Automate the press line and eliminate human error.*
   b. _____
   c. _____
2. a. *Increase service hours available by 50%*
   b. *Decrease service response time to not more than 3 hours.*
   c. _____
3. a. _____
   b. _____
   c. _____

3

You, the planning coordinator, should complete the **Level 3** Corporate Objectives page and be certain that all affected persons have a copy of it. A blank copy is in the appendix.

Also, give each participant a copy of the **Level 3** Planning Process Assumptions page, found in the appendix.

CORPORATE OBJECTIVES

Who: Although this sounds repetitive, the fact is that the same people from **Level 1** should also be responsible here.

What: The U.S. Marine Corps advertises for *a few good men*. We believe you need *a few good objectives*. How many? There are no hard and fast rules but the number four seems reasonable. Often, two objectives are expressed in financial statement terms (e.g., profitability, return on assets, return on sales, gross margin, cost reduction, net worth, return on stockholders' equity). One is employee oriented (training, benefits, work environment, etc.); the other is project oriented (new plan, new territory, new product, etc.).

However many objectives you choose to state, each should be:

• Specific	• Clear	• Positive
• Measurable	• Concise	• Reasonable
• Actionable	• Consistent	• Inclusive
• Relevant	• Motivating	• Timebound

When: You may be able to add this onto the **Level 2** meeting. However, we suggest that you not do that on your first attempt at building a plan. You need time to ratify **Level 1** and **Level 2** before setting your objectives. Therefore, we suggest a delay of two to four weeks following **Level 2**.

Where: If time and/or money is a problem this can be done on-site. However, we recommend going off-site if possible.

How Long: Depending upon the clarity of the strategic plan, this may take only one day. Plan on arriving at midday and departing late the following afternoon. Again, however, while the process may culminate in one day, it will percolate over several weeks.

The following pages in this section can be used to help with the formulation of the plan. You may choose to complete some of them yourself or to give them to others to complete.

HISTORY QUESTIONNAIRE

This is basic information for the plan—particularly for those recipients of the plan who are new to the company or are outsiders. You may want more historical information or you may find different historical data for different parts of the company—particularly those which have been acquired.

The basic question is "How did we get to be who we are today?"

HISTORY QUESTIONNAIRE

To be completed by: _Sam Someone_

   Completing these questions will help to show how we became what we are and why we are positioned to do what we have planned to do.

1. Date of company's founding _____

    _____

2. Original founder(s) of business, name of business, location of business, and purpose of business _____

    _____

3. Changes in name, location, and/or purpose, along with corresponding dates. _____

    _____

    _____

4. Major economic or environmental events which have affected company. _____

    _____ _1982 Recession in mining —_ _____

    EPA crackdown on toxic emissions

5. Dates and explanations of major additions to or divestitures of business. _____

    _____

    _____

6. Major obstacles and problems the business has faced. _____

    Environmental cleanup in 1983.

    _____

7. Turning points, and causes of greatest periods of growth and profitability. _____

    _____ _1974 energy shortage_ _____

    _____

EVALUATION CHART FOR PLANNING

This sheet, which has an instruction page with it in the appendix, is intended as a means to stimulate communications. From it you should be able to develop some objectives. Additional helpful forms included are:

- Where Are We?

- Where Are We Going?

- Status Quo Questionnaire

- How Do We Get There?

- How Do We Know When We Are There?

Review each of these sheets. Ask yourself who can provide the most information by considering and answering these questions. Probably, you will want to give these to everyone involved at **Level 3** and ask them to complete the sheets before coming to the meeting. There is a blank form, with suggestions, in the appendix.

EVALUATION CHART FOR PLANNING

Areas	Communications			Capital Investment											
ELEMENTS	Clarity of Instructions			Production Equipment	Vehicles										
100															
95															
90															
85				■											
80															
75	■														
70															
65															
60															
55															
50															
45															
40															
35															
30				■											
25															
20															
15															
10															
5															

Instructions: For those elements of which you have knowledge, mark the appropriate square to give a score which answers the question "How are we doing with respect to this element?"

The several pages following are primarily for your benefit as the plan coordinator. They will help you divide the relevant questions into workable pieces. You may want to reserve these questions and ask them in the planning session.

However, if you want to get written answers, copies of the pages are included in the appendix.

WHERE ARE WE?

To be completed by: _____

1. Why are we in business?

   _____

2. What business are we in?

   _____

3. Where are we in the life cycle of the industry?

   _____

4. Where are we in the life cycle of the company?

   _____

5. How did we get here?

   _____

   a. Narrative background of major events

      _____

   b. Historical financial information

      _____

6. What market factors affect us?

   _____

   a. Input side
      • Personnel

      _____

      • Materials

      _____

- Financing

_____

- Equipment

_____

b. Output side
- Primary customers

_____

- Secondary customers

_____

7. What internal factors affect us?

_____

a. Our strengths

_____

b. Our weaknesses

_____

8. What other external factors affect us?

_____

a. Regulation

_____

b. Legislation

_____

c. Competition

_____

WHERE ARE WE GOING?

To be completed by: _____

1. Who are the *we* referred to above?

   _____

2. What alternatives are available to us?

   _____

3. Consider the critical issues such as:

   a. Desired rate of growth

      _____

   b. Desired rate of profitability

      _____

   c. Desired public image

      _____

   d. New markets

      _____

   e. New products

      _____

   f. Availability of financing

      _____

   g. Capability of personnel

      _____

   h. Adequacy of plant and equipment

      _____

4. Where will our strengths take us?

   _____

5. What are our priorities?

   _____

STATUS QUO QUESTIONNAIRE

To be completed by: _____

1. If the company operates in the coming year in the same manner as this year, identify those areas under your budgeting control (budget lines) which:

   a. Must be increased

   _____

   b. Could stay the same

   _____

   c. Are targets for cost reductions

   _____

2. Again assuming the present methods of operations:

   a. Identify two conditions over which you have little control that keep your area from making a greater profit contribution.

   _____

   _____

   b. State two changes which you have (or can get) authority to change that should make your area more profitable.

   _____

   _____

   c. By what date(s) could the above changes reasonably be made?

   _____

HOW DO WE GET THERE?

To be completed by: _____

1. What alternative courses are available to us?

   _____

2. What are the pros and cons of each alternative?

   _____

3. Which alternatives match up with our resources and our strengths (path of least resistance)?

   _____

4. What option(s) gives us the greatest future advantage?

   _____

5. Which objective is first priority?

   _____

6. Who will be responsible for each identified course of action?

   _____

7. What time frames should each have?

   _____

8. What is the biggest stumbling block to achieving our objective? Can we break it into more manageable problems?

   _____

9. What major external economic events (devaluations, political overthrows, nationalization, recessions, etc.) do we foresee?

   _____

10. What major internal economic events (acquisitions, divestitures, retirements, product demise, etc.) do we foresee?

    _____

11. What will it cost—dollars, people, dedication, etc.?

    _____

12. Do we have checkpoints and evacuation routes established?

_____

13. Is it consistent with our strategic plan?

_____

14. Can we monitor and measure our progress?

_____

15. Does this fit our stated philosophy?

_____

HOW DO WE KNOW WHEN WE ARE THERE?

To be completed by: _____

1. Do you have a means to quantify your objectives and goals to the maximum extent possible?

   _____

2. Do you have controls built into the planning process?

   _____

3. Can you describe the final product in sufficient detail so that others can clearly picture what you are attempting to accomplish?

   _____

4. Is the performance measure agreed upon?

   _____

The next two lists can be used in several ways:

1. You can use them yourself as a means of directing provoking questions during the meetings to ensure that everyone is fully thinking through his/her suggestions.

2. You can assign a particular person the responsibility of following up on each objective.

3. You can disperse the lists to the participants as a guide.

Each of these procedures has proven successful in different environments. Were we to choose only one, we would choose the third.

PLANNING THE REPORTS

1. Show the plan
2. Show the actual
3. Show the difference
4. Show period and year to date
5. Determine when to require explanations
6. Explanations include:

    a. Who is responsible?

    b. What caused it?

    c. Should it continue?

    d. What is to be done?

    e. When will it be done?

    f. Should the plan be changed? When?

PLANNING THE CONTROLS

1. What is to happen?
2. When should it happen?
3. When and how will we know if it is going to happen?
4. When and how will we know if it has happened?
5. Can we divide it into a series of events?
6. Are there points where we can reconsider?
7. Who is responsible for making it happen?
8. Who reports?
9. Are reports quantifiable?
10. Are reports verifiable?
11. What are the tolerances?

The Internal Data Monitoring sheet is an example of information you may want to collect as a part of the planning process. The Desired Pro Forma column may present some objectives (or at least unit goals) that you will establish.

Collect the information in the first two columns and fill them in. Give the sheets to the participants and collectively determine what the numbers in the last column should be for the upcoming period.

If you desire, you can extend the pro forma for more periods.

INTERNAL DATA MONITORING

Item Monitored	Last Period	Current Period	Desired Pro Forma
Financial			
1. Profit Margin (Earnings/Sales)	.04	.037	.0425
2. Asset Turnover (Sales/Assets)	3.5	3.3	3.6
3. Capital Structure (Assets/Equity)	2.2	2.9	2.1
4. Return on Equity [(1) × (2) × (3)]			
5. Accounts Receivable Turnover (Sales/Accounts Receivable)			
6. Accounts Payable Turnover (Purchases/Accounts Payable)			
7. Current Ratio (Current Assets/Current Liabilities)			
Operational*			
8.			
9.			

*Examples of operational data to be monitored might include:

- Backlog
- Down-time
- Rejects
- Calls received

The following two pages in this section represent a small sample of the kinds of information that is easily available and can be helpful in the planning process.

Of course, these lists are by no means exhaustive but they can help you find some data of interest.

You may want to make these lists, with additions of particular importance to your industry and/or company, available to everyone involved in the planning process.

SOURCES OF EXTERNAL INFORMATION

Federal Government

1. Statistical Abstract of the United States
   (U.S. Department of Commerce, Bureau of the Census)
   Issued Annually
   Social, Political, and Economic Statistics

2. Survey of Current Business
   (U.S. Department of Commerce, Bureau of Economic Analysis)
   Issued Monthly
   Business Indicators, Domestic & Foreign Trade, Prices, Labor & Employment, Raw Materials

3. Economic Indicators
   (Superintendent of Documents, Government Printing Office)
   Issued Monthly

4. Bureau of Census has several publications which are very helpful with demographics but most are issued on a ten-year cycle.

5. Federal Reserve Bulletin
   (Board of Governors of the Federal Reserve System)
   Issued Monthly

State Governments
State departments of commerce have data with a more local and regional orientation. They can be especially helpful in gathering information on the availability and price of labor.

COMPUTER ACCESSIBLE DATA BASES

1. Data Courier, Inc., Louisville, Kentucky
   ABI/INFORM

2. The Center for Vocational Education, Ohio State University, Columbus, Ohio
   AIM/ARM

3. Arthur D. Little Decision Resources, Cambridge, Massachusetts
   Arthur D. Little/Online

4. Business International Corporation, New York, New York
   BI/DATA Forecasts
   BI/DATA Timeseries

5. Bureau of Labor Statistics, United States Department of Labor, Washington, D.C.
   BLS Consumer Price Index
   BLS Employment, Hours, and Earnings
   BLS Labor Force
   BLS Producer Price Index

6. Dun's Marketing Services, Parsippany, New Jersey
   D&B Dun's Market Identifiers 10+
   D&B Million Dollar Directory
   D&B Principal International Business

7. Disclosure Incorporated, Bethesda, Maryland
   Disclosure II

8. Gale Research Company, Detroit, Michigan
   Encyclopedia of Associations

9. Reports and Studies Index, Find/SVP, New York, New York
   Find/SVP

10. Bureau of National Affairs, Inc., Washington, D.C.
    Laborlaw

11. Predicasts, Inc., Cleveland, Ohio
    PTS Annual Reports Abstracts
    PTS F&S Indexes
    PTS International Forecasts
    PTS International Timeseries
    PTS Prompt
    PTS U.S. Forecasts
    PTS U.S. Timeseries

12. United States Department of Commerce, Washington, D.C.
    U.S. Exports
    Trade Opportunities

Trade Associations

Besides periodicals and published studies, personal contact can be helpful here. Prepublication information and even that which is not to be published is sometimes available.

Trade Publications

These publications are especially helpful for their (usually) annual statistical issues.

USING FORCE-FIELD ANALYSIS TO ACCOMPLISH OBJECTIVES

Using force-field analysis to accomplish objectives is an idea for you, the planning coordinator. During the meeting at **Level 3** you may want to consider using the approach outlined on this page.

Force-field analysis, reduced to its simplest form, states that when movement from one condition to another is desired, two sets of forces operate: pressing and restraining. Many times, the easiest way to bring about movement is to remove restraining forces rather than merely pressing harder.

To use this approach:

1. Identify objectives.

2. Identify restraining forces for each objective.

3. Group restraining forces by categories.

4. Find ways to remove or reduce restraining forces and categories, beginning with the weakest.

5. Set target dates for completion and name persons responsible.

6. Have follow-up meetings and/or reports soon after the target dates.

7. Do the above for the pressing forces.

With all of the information gathered so far the biggest problem may be to condense all of the possible, worthwhile objectives into just a few. We suggest you get down to not more than five (we prefer four).

These five (or fewer) should be:

• Specific	• Clear	• Positive
• Measurable	• Concise	• Reasonable
• Actionable	• Consistent	• Inclusive
• Relevant	• Motivating	• Timebound

Remember, objectives should be written in such a way that every planning unit can state one or more goals directly in support of the objective. Test each objective statement against the above list and rewrite it until it meets all the requirements.

Now you are ready to review the philosophy and mission, strategic plan, and objectives. If these are all consistent and stated as senior management wants them to be, distribute this information to all who will participate in **Level 4**.

Ask for feedback and be sure to give them a specific time. Modify any of these, if necessary, and give the **Level 4** people an approved set of this information before they start work at **Level 4**.

4

Level 4 is that portion of the process where the planning gets down to the nitty-gritty. Until now, senior management has been contemplating the accomplishment of the company as a whole. Some of the ends that have been espoused may appear exceptionally difficult and unlikely if not impossible.

At this point, the various responsibility units of the company (we call them planning units) divide the objectives into we-can-do-it pieces called goals. Goals are objectives divided into specific responsibility segments.

At the conclusion of the Level 4 process you should have a list of goals which, when put together, add up to the overall objectives.

If the objectives have been well written, all (or almost all) of the planning units will be able to state at least one goal in support of each objective. If this is not the case, the goals should be reconsidered. If the goals seem appropriate, the objectives may need to be rewritten.

As in the earlier levels, appropriate forms are included in the appendix.

PLANNING UNIT GOALS

Who: Generally, those who directly report to those involved with Level 1 will be the main focus of this level (i.e., product managers, territory managers, plant managers, division managers, etc.).

What: Each planning unit should state at least one goal in support of each corporate objective. The real burden at Level 3 is to develop objectives that are truly corporate and into which every planning unit can reasonably fit. Each goal should be a component block of accomplishing the objective that it supports.

When: The first three levels should be complete and should have been disseminated to these people before they begin work on Level 4. We suggest a minimum period of two weeks for feedback from these people after the products of Level 1 through Level 3 have been given to them. Once senior management is comfortable that Level 1 through Level 3 are reasonably solid, work can begin on Level 4.

Where: Separate meetings will first be held by individual planning units to construct their own goals. These should take place on-site because of the numbers and job requirements of the people. Once the planning units have developed their goals, the planning unit managers should meet for one day in an off-site setting to present their goals to each other for discussion, revision (if necessary), and adoption. Of course, it is important that the adopted and approved goals add up to the accomplishment of the objectives. If they do not, either the goals or the objectives must be modified to make them all align.

How Long: As indicated above, there may be several different meetings of varying lengths involved here. Total elapsed time will often be about four weeks.

Obviously, your starting spot for consideration of appropriate planning unit goals is the information developed in **Level 1** through **Level 3**. You should distribute this information to the planning unit managers as quickly as possible. Prepare a small package that includes the philosophy and mission, the strategic plan, and the objectives. You may also want to include information upon which these are based.

Request written feedback on these documents by a specified date. If any significant problems with these documents are noted, reconvene the appropriate people to review and revise as necessary.

When the **Level 1** through **Level 3** output has been confirmed, distribute the authorized version to the planning units and instruct them that this is the foundation for their planning effort.

Be certain that each planning unit manager gets at least one Planning Unit Goal Sheet for each objective set in **Level 3**. You will expect them to complete and return at least one such sheet for each objective. You may choose to type the objective on the sheets for them. If so, be sure to put only one objective per page.

Note there are three sample Planning Unit Goal Sheets near the end of this section.

Also included in this section are several sample analysis sheets. (In the appendix you will find clean copies followed by instructions for each.) Choose those which you think will be helpful to your people and give them to the planning unit managers as a part of the package you prepare as the authorized version of **Level 1** through **Level 3**.

If you are considering a planning retreat for your people, the next two pages may be helpful. They are intended as general guidance only and should be modified to meet your needs.

PLANNING THE PLAN

A Planning Retreat Schedule
(A **Level 4** Example)

—— Day 1 ——

TIME*	ACTIVITY
One hour	Evaluation Chart for Planning completed: general historical review of company, major emphasis on past year's performance with comparisons to expectations
Two hours	Explanations of variances from expectations (confined to not more than 15 minutes per reporting division)
Two hours	Moderator summarizes Evaluation Chart for Planning results and promotes discussion and consensus; summarizes the above to focus attention on common problems and opportunities
One hour	Moderated discussion of anticipations of external events affecting business during planning horizon
Two hours	Subgroup meetings to establish unit goals for coming period.

—— Day 2 ——

TIME*	ACTIVITY
Two hours	Each subgroup presents its unit goals for the next period (not more than 15 minutes each)
One hour	Moderator leads discussion to find goal congruence and conflicts—each is listed
One hour	Moderator leads discussion to align and prioritize goals as agreed
Three hours	Based upon consensus goals, subgroups meet to determine and coordinate tactics and resource needs
One hour	Moderator summarizes above and seeks consensus; goals, tactics, and resource needs will be compiled into *Business Plan* for review

* Times are, of course, approximate. You may choose not to publish the time schedule to participants, but the coordinator should have time estimates from which to work.

INPUT FACTORS ANALYSIS

Item	Information	Indicator	Source
Personnel: • Management • Technical • Supervisory • Production • Support	Availability of people in area qualified for entry level repair job.	Number of people graduating with AA or BA in Computer Science.	Placement offices of the following schools: a. b. c.
Financing: • Long-term Debt • Long-term Equity • Short-term			
Materials:			
Equipment:			

administration

Planning Unit

To be completed by: *P. Manager*

INPUT FACTORS ANTICIPATION

Item _____ *K4776 Interchange Control*

Annual Quantity _____ *180,000*

Seasonal Variations _____ *Jan. – Jun. 10,000/month; Jul. – Sept. 30,000/month; Oct. – Dec. 10,000/month*

Acceptable Substitute _____ *K4776-B Interchange Knob*

	Sources	
	Primary: *Control Ind.*	Secondary: *Precision Knobs*
Price Range	*$ 1.47 each*	*$ 1.49 each*
Lead Time	*7 weeks*	*6 weeks*
Availability	*Constant*	*Sporadic*

Anticipated Effects of Using Secondary Source or Substitute:

Costs *additional 2¢ each for secondary — overprices competition*

Quality *not as good — 20% higher failure rate*

Sales/Marketing *Changes product appearance*

Production *no effect*

Personnel *no effect except quality assurance*

Planning Unit _____ *Sales*

To be completed by: _____ *S. Manager*

OUTPUT FACTORS ANTICIPATION

	Ours	1	2	3	4	5
Price Range:						
Previous Year 1987	4.00 – 4.25					
Current Year 1988	4.10 – 4.25					
New Year 1989	4.15 – 4.30					
Annual Quantity:						
Previous Year 1987	127,000					
Current Year 1988	129,000					
Next Year 1989	141,000					

Describe Anticipated Changes in:

Total Market _____ Slow increase in total

Market Share _____ Hold our own or lose slightly

Number of Competitors _____ One as two new entrants with deep pockets behind them

Product Substitutes _____ None seen

Advertising Levels _____ Same

Customers _____ Same

Planning Unit _Manufacturing_

To be completed by: _M. Manager_

PRODUCT PLANNING RECORD

Product _X-lon_   For Year of 19 _88_

		Year				
		1986	1987	1988 Present	1989	1990
1) Units Sold	—Actual	297 K	325 K	450 K		
2)	—Projected	400 K	450 K	475 K	500 K	550 K
3) Unit Sales Price	—Actual	3.86	3.89	3.97		
4)	—Projected	3.75	3.82	3.94	4.05	4.09
5) Unit Variable Cost	—Actual					
6)	—Projected					
7) Unit Gross Margin	—Actual					
8)	—Projected					
9) Total Revenue	—Actual					
10)	—Projected					
11) Promotion Expense	—Actual					
12)	—Projected					
13)						
14)						
15)						
16)						

Problems may be indicated by:

- Declining number of units sold
- Declining total revenue
- Declining margins

- Increasing price reductions to maintain sales
- Increasing costs as a percent of sales

- Increasing promotion expense as a percent of sales
- Significant variances between actuals and projections

81

Planning Unit _Sales_

To be completed by: _Each Salesman_

SALESPERSON'S SALES FORECAST FOR 19 _89_

Jones & Co.   _H. Man_

Customer   Salesman

| | Units Projected | | | | |
Product(s)	Quarter 1	Quarter 2	Quarter 3	Quarter 4	Annual
X-Lon	400	425	550	400	1775
Y-Lon	375	390	375	450	1590
N-Lon	-0-	100	400	-0-	500
Totals	775	915	1325	850	3865

- Summarize by division
- Summarize by product

Planning Unit _Sales_

To be completed by: _Each Salesman_

SALES FORECAST SUMMARY FOR 19_89_

Product(s)	Units Projected				
	Quarter 1	Quarter 2	Quarter 3	Quarter 4	Annual
X-Lion	4,000	4,500	7,000	4,500	20,000
Y-Lion	3,900	4,000	4,100	3,900	15,900
N-Lion	4,100	4,000	4,500	4,000	16,600
Totals	12,000	12,500	15,600	12,400	52,500

Planning Unit _____ *marketing*

To be completed by: _____ *M. Manager*

VALUE ANALYSIS GRID

Value

Product/Service _____ *A*

A value analysis grid plotting price (vertical axis, from "Lowest Price in Market" to "Highest Price in Market") against quality (horizontal axis, from "Lowest Quality in Market" to "Highest Quality in Market"), with a diagonal "Value Line." Plotted points: "Worst Value" (top left), "Our Company" (top right), "Competitor 4" (upper middle), "Competitor 2" (middle), "Competitor 3" (right), "Competitor 1" (lower left), and "Best Value" (bottom right).

Competitor 3 may be a formidable opponent. They are equal to our quality but at a lower price. We will be very concerned with how they got there and whether a price war is about to break out. Do they have lower costs or are they sacrificing margins?

How did competitor 4 get where it is? Are they resting on reputation or did they get a perception of higher quality (and therefore price) through advertising?

Planning Unit _____marketing_____

To be completed by: _____M. Manager_____

VALUE ANALYSIS GRID

Product/Service _____B_____

Highest Price in Market — Worst Value				Our Company	Competitor 4
				Competitor 2	Competitor 3
Competitor 1					
Lowest Price in Market					Best Value

Lowest Quality in Market ... Highest Quality in Market

Value Line

This is obviously a *high end* product. Probably Competitor 1 is doing a knock-off and is capitalizing on the prestige of the product look-alike for those who can't or won't afford the real thing.

Again, a determination of how we got where we are and whether we want to be there is quite important.

The sheet below is the end product of **Level 4** planning. Each planning unit should complete at least one such sheet for each objective stated in **Level 3**.

PLANNING UNIT GOAL SHEET

Objective _____ _____

_____

Goal _____ _____

_____

Present Status (/   /   )

_____

_____

_____

Resource Requirements

_____

_____

_____

Responsible Individual _____

Estimated Completion Date _____

Concurring Managers _____ _____

Authorized Approval _____

Comments _____

_____

_____

_____

Note the example sheets following.

The goals stated on these sheets should support the specific objective to which they are related, and as previously noted for the objectives, they should be:

• Specific	• Clear	• Positive
• Measurable	• Concise	• Reasonable
• Actionable	• Consistent	• Inclusive
• Relevant	• Motivating	• Timebound

Goals and objectives should be both doable and worth doing. It is the *so what?* test. If the objective or goal is accomplished and someone can still say "So what?", perhaps there isn't enough stretch in them.

Goals which don't have some resource requirements with them may indicate:

1. The goal is trivial.

2. The person doesn't understand what it will take to get the job done.

3. The unit is fat and has resources that aren't currently being used.

Any of the above suggest management should look closely at the area.

PLANNING UNIT GOAL SHEET

Example 1

Objective _____ _Introduce X-Tron into three market territories by May 30, 1989_

Goal _Marketing_ _Achieve a 15% awareness of X-Tron product on the standard "0" survey by Jan. 30, 1989_

Present Status (6 / 30 / 88)

A before survey has been conducted and the awareness level now is approximately 3 percent.

Resource Requirements

$125,000 budget for media, literature, and trade shows

Responsible Individual _Marketing Support Manager_

Estimated Completion Date _January 30, 1989_

Concurring Managers _Sales Manager_

Authorized Approval _____

Comments _Because we already have products in these markets, we can coattail an existing market/sales contracts and literature._

PLANNING UNIT GOAL SHEET

Example 2

Objective _____ net income before tax of $2.3 MM for fiscal 1989

Goal _Product 3_ $20 million gross sales at 30 percent gross margin

Present Status (6 / 1 / 88)

Last year's sales were $18 million and margins were 27 percent. This was a period of penetration in two markets. Those markets are maturing and should yield slightly greater margins because our product is now proven.

Resource Requirements

Our primary need is for better literature. We must maintain our media campaign, even stepping it up slightly, and we need four-color literature to leave with prospects. Upgrade one sales position to sales manager.

Responsible Individual _Sales Manager — Product 3_

Estimated Completion Date _End of year_

Concurring Managers _Marketing Manager_

Authorized Approval _____

Comments _This product fits our historic trends with product/market mix. There is no reason to expect it to deviate much from our norm. Our goal represents an 11 percent increase in sales and an 11 percent improvement in margins._

PLANNING UNIT GOAL SHEET

Example 3

Objective _____ *Enhance each employee's job satisfaction skills*

Goal *Manufacturing* *Each department employee will successfully pass all skills tests on the Auto/Spot machine.*

Present Status (*6* / *30* / *88*)

The department recently acquired the Auto/Spot welding machine. No employee has yet been trained to use it.

Resource Requirements

One person will be dedicated full time as the trainer until all department employees have been trained.

Responsible Individual *Foreman*

Estimated Completion Date *June 15, 1989*

Concurring Managers *None*

Authorized Approval _____

Comments *This equipment will become the standard over the next three years.*

If each planning unit has completed one or more goal sheets for each objective you should have a substantial list of things to be accomplished.

Some planning units may have goals that do not specifically attach to any objective. These should be minimized and should be subject to more careful consideration than ones which do support objectives.

Remember, one of the aims is to focus the resources of the business on a few essential objectives in order to improve the probability of accomplishing them. Goals not in support of an objective tend to dissipate resources.

Collect the Goal Sheets from all planning units. Arrange them by objective (all goals that support objective 1, etc.)

On the Outline of Planned Changes sheet list the goals by objective. Complete all columns.

1. Do the goals listed for each objective accumulate to assure the accomplishment of that objective? If not, either *stretch* some of the goals or *downsize* the objective.

2. Consider whether the results of the goals are worth the costs. If not, modify the goal or the means of accomplishing it accordingly.

3. Consider the timelines. Are they reasonable? Will they do what you need by when you need it?

Feed back any changes to the planning unit managers. Planning unit managers will use these approved goals as the basis for **Level 5**.

OUTLINE OF

#	Goals	Expected Results	$
1	Increase Productivity	5% decrease in Direct Labor	1MM

PLANNED CHANGES

Resources Required	$	Timelines			
		1st Qtr.	2nd Qtr.	3rd Qtr.	4th Qtr.
1 Press	500K	/ —————————— /			

You, the plan coordinator, should have returned the Goal Sheets, revised as necessary, to the planning unit managers. Any substantive revision to the sheets should, of course, have been discussed with the manager as well.

You may also want to give copies of all Goal Sheets to all planning unit managers in order to keep them informed of the overall plan.

Once the planning unit managers have their approved goals back, it is time for them to complete the detailed action plans that go along with the goals. Obviously, the managers had at least a general plan of attack when they developed the goal. Now it is time to finalize that process.

You will want to give them blank copies of the Goal Action Plan Sheet (found in the appendix), as well as the completed examples included in this section. You will expect each manager to return a Goal Action Plan Sheet for each of their goals.

TACTICS AND PROJECTIONS

Who: The planning unit managers and their direct reports (this may go down to the first line supervisors).

What: Each adopted and approved goal should have an action plan with appropriate measurements and monitoring points for it. Since this is the *daily operational portion* of the plan, it will be detailed.

When: Work can commence on this level as soon as senior management has approved the product of **Level 4**.

Where: Because of the information needed and because of the numbers and job requirements of the people involved, these meetings will probably be held on-site.

How Long: There will likely be many short (1–3 hours) meetings involved in the development of this part of the plan. Total elapsed time again may be about four weeks.

Examples of the Goal Action Plan forms for the planning unit follow. These forms should indicate how, when, and at what cost the planning unit goals will be accomplished.

Each *Tactic* or *Action Step* assigned to an individual should also show up on that person's Individual Accountability and Action Plan sheets.

GOAL ACTION PLAN SHEET

Example 1

1987

#	Tactics/Action Steps	Responsible Person	Status/Comments	Projections/Evidence of Completion	J	F	M	A	M	J	J	A	S	O	N	D
1	Tabulate results of before survey	JJ		Tabulation complete	X											
2	Formulate market plan from (1)	JJ/AS		Plan submitted to PJ and approved		X	—	X								
3	Complete new media spot	BC	$40 K	Spot placed 3 times					X							
4	Complete new literature	BC	$35 K	Literature in hands of sales people						X						
5	Attend 3 regional trade shows	JJ	$42 K	Show attended/list submitted					X			X		X		
6	Conduct "Q" survey	JJ/Agency	$8 K	Survey complete w/15% awareness												X

Goal _Marketing Support Dept._

Report Date	J	F	M	A	M	J	J	A	S	O	N	D
Date												
Initials												

GOAL ACTION PLAN SHEET

Example 2

#	Tactics/Action Steps	Responsible Person	Status/Comments	Projections/Evidence of Completion	J	F	M	A	M	J	J	A	S	O	N	D
1	Trainer trained	MM		Certificate of completion	X											
2	Training manual completed	MM/Trainer Personnel		Book approved— Personnel		X	—	X								
3	On-the-job checklist	Trainer/ Personnel		Checklist approved— Personnel				X								
4	Class 1—15 people	Trainer		Completed classroom					X							
5	O-J-T Class 1	Trainer		Certificates							X—X					
6	Class 2—15 people	Trainer		Completed classroom							X—X					
7	O-J-T Class 2	Trainer		Certificates									X—X			
8	Class 3—10 people	Trainer		Completed classroom									X—X			
9	O-J-T Class 3	Trainer		Certificates											X—X	
10	Dept. celebration	MM/Trainer		Party												X

Goal *Manufacturing — Welding Dept.*

	J	F	M	A	M	J	J	A	S	O	N	D
Report Date												
Date												
Initials												

GOAL ACTION PLAN SHEET

Example 3

#	Tactics/Action Steps	Responsible Person	Status/Comments	Projections/Evidence of Completion	J	F	M	A	M	J	J	A	S	O	N	D
1	Complete new product literature	PT/Lj		Available to field		X										
2	Identify new sales mgr. prospect	PT		List of 3 to personnel				X								
3	Select sales mgr.	PT		Position filled					X							
4	Sales mgr. trained	PT/MK		Accepted evaluation							X —— X					
5	Implement new price list	Sales Mgr.		Mailed to customers									X			
6	Year-end-sales event	Sales Mgr.		Promotion complete										X		
7	Sales bonus bacol	Sales Mgr.		Awards made										X — X		
8	Non-discount customers target program	Sales Mgr.		50 new non-discount customers												X

Goal *Product 3 — Sales Dept.*

	Report Date	J	F	M	A	M	J	J	A	S	O	N	D
	Date												
	Initials												

INDIVIDUAL ACCOUNTABILITY AND ACTION PLANS

Name _John Doe_

Position _Salesman_

Evaluator _H. Man_ Date _____

Approved by _____ Date _____

Individual Accountability:

1. Improve territory unit sales by 10%

Individual Action Items:

1. Prepare customer prospect list.
2. Make at least 3 cold calls per week.
3.

Measurements:

1. List to H. Man by 1/15
2. Sales log

Performance Evaluation of Accountability:

( ) More than
Satisfactory   ( ) Satisfactory   ( ) Less than
Satisfactory

INDIVIDUAL PERFORMANCE EVALUATION

Name _____ *John Doe* _____

Position _____ *Salesman* _____

Dates of Review Period ____/____/____ to ____/____/____

Summary of Performance Evaluation:
( ) More than   (**X**) Satisfactory   ( ) Less than
Satisfactory   Satisfactory

Too New to Evaluate:

( ) Satisfactory Progress   ( ) Unsatisfactory Progress

Action Plan Summary: (Use additional sheets if necessary)

Strong Points _____ *Good planning and detail* _____

_____

Weak Points _____ *Follow-up on service problems* _____

_____

Plan for Development _____ *Enroll in Service School.* _____

_____

Evaluator's Signature _____ Date _____

Approved by _____ Date _____

Accountabilities Established:

( ) Accountabilities have been established for the upcoming period.

Evaluator's Signature _____ Date _____

Approved by _____ Date _____

6

With the exception of the budget and related financial information, the business plan should now be essentially complete—at least in terms of raw input information.

We have left out the budget area. Companies large enough to have a full-time accounting staff probably already have some form of budget (or have the expertise to develop one). Smaller companies may need outside help to get this done.

In any case, the formats by which budgets are developed vary tremendously and can't be adequately covered here. We recommend you find a good budgeting book if this is an area with which you need help.

However, we do emphasize that all of the work we described up to now should be completed before the budget is done. The *plan should drive the budget*, not the reverse.

Following is the Business Plan Outline with additional explanatory material. You may want to use this to put the document together. When you have gathered all of the paper from the first five levels you should see the basis of your plan.

COORDINATION

Who: When it comes to completing the plan it is usually best to have one person designated to put it into document form. Whoever is so designated should have sufficient clout to require and obtain cooperation to get parts of the plan in as needed.

What: A written document following the outline given earlier. If possible, the basic text portion of the plan should be about 20 pages. The appendices may be as voluminous as necessary to support the plan.

When: The plan should be complete and in the hands of all responsible people 15 to 30 days before it is to become the operative document.

Where: Normally, the plan is completed (put together) in the office environment.

How Long: Finalization should not really be a large problem if the preceding steps have been well followed. Allow at least two weeks, and preferably four, to put the document together.

BUSINESS PLAN OUTLINE

1. Cover Sheet: With appropriate descriptions

   a. Business name

   b. Business address

   c. Business phone

   d. Principals

   e. Date

2. Sign-up: Signature of all contributors to the plan.

3. Executive Summary: This is what sells someone on reading the remainder of the plan. It should be one or two pages in length and contain the essence of the plan.

   a. For whom is it written?

   b. What is being requested from them?

   c. Why should they be interested in doing it?

4. Table of Contents: Be specific and complete in this area. Some readers may judge the completeness of the plan from the details provided in the table of contents.

5. Major Assumptions: Any planning process creates assumptions upon which certain goals and action plans are premised. Assumptions which are key to the plan should be stated and emergency contingency steps should be formulated for assumptions that may be violated.

6. History Section: If this is a start-up venture, a brief explanation of how the idea (company) came to be is in order at this point. If this is an operating plan, the history section may have the major highlights supplemented with additional details in an appendix.

7. Philosophy: This is taken directly from the work done in **Level 1**. Some people prefer not to publish the philosophy. We suggest you do, as this helps solidify the company around a common set of beliefs.

8. Definition of the Business: It is important that you be able to state succinctly what the business is. This is distinct from what the business does (a listing of functions, products, or services) and is oriented to answering the questions:

   a. What do we do best?

   b. What need does that meet?

   c. Who has that need?

9. Definition of the Market: Markets are composed of buyers and sellers. This section should include some discussion of each. The discussion of buyers could focus on the questions: Who buys and why do they buy? A description of the customer or client base and the factors considered important in the buying decision by them would be appropriate. With respect to sellers, a listing of competitors and a ranking of those competitors with respect to factors held important in the minds of buyers would be helpful. Expectations of changes in market penetration by the company and its competitors should be included.

10. Description of Products or Services: The identified need and the identified market will be accommodated by specific products or services. The description(s) of the products or services should fully explain to the reader why, given the previously stated information, such products or services will be demanded. You may append catalog sheets, pictures, etc.

11. Management Structure: Having described the business, the market, and the product, it is time to indicate who will make things happen. A start-up or financing plan will require more details than will an operating plan. Résumés and other details of the personal backgrounds should be left to an appendix. This section should sell two things: *that you have the right people* and *that they are properly organized*.

12. Strategies, Objectives, Goals, and Tactics: What you intend to accomplish and how. This section will include varying amounts of details based upon the purpose of the plan, but it is important to focus on the *crunch factors*. The detail should be placed in individual appendices. Items to be covered in this section include:

    a. Sales forecasts

    b. Marketing plans

    c. Manufacturing plans

    d. Quality assurance plans

    e. Financial plans

13. Financial Data: The plan is future oriented. Therefore, this section should focus on projections and pro formas. Historical financial information necessary to understanding the plan should be referenced in an appendix. The items to be included are:

    a. Cost-volume-profit analysis

    b.   Income projections—pro forma

- Monthly for planning year
- Quarterly for second year
- Annual for third year

    c.   Cash flow analysis—pro forma

- Monthly for planning year
- Quarterly for second year
- Annual for third year

    d.   Break-even analysis

    e.   Annual pro forma balance sheets

14. Appendices: These give supporting detail to the content section as well as adding material of interest not otherwise included. If there is proprietary information (patent, research and development, formulas, market research, etc.) that you may wish to control, it would be well to place that information into detachable appendices.

    a.   Narrative history of the company

    b.   Management structure, additional résumés, organization charts, etc.

    c.   Details of objectives, goals, and tactics

- Products and services
- Research and development
- Marketing
- Manufacturing
- Administration
- Finance

    d.   Historical financial information (3–5 years if possible)

    e.   Tax returns (3–5 years if possible)

    f.   Letters of recommendation or endorsement

    g.   Contingency plans

    h.   Change process

Well, the plan is done. Almost!

As surely as you spent time and effort, blood and tears putting this together, some things will change. And when they do, the plan must be flexible enough to recognize the changes and adapt where necessary.

For that reason we have included the following Plan Change Process. This is a sample which you should modify to meet your needs. And the page should be kept current so everyone will have an up-to-date version of the plan.

PLAN CHANGE PROCESS

This plan will be reviewed quarterly by its preparers. The review meeting will be held in the *third* week after the end of the quarter. The meeting will be called and the location, time, and agenda set by *H. Man* .

Included in the agenda will be:

1. A review of results obtained

2. A review of assumptions

3. A review of performance vs. plan

4. Suggested changes

Those having suggestions for additional agenda items should submit them at least one week before the meeting.

Changes approved in the meeting will be included in the plan book with changes to appropriate pages.

Date of Change	Pages Changed	Reasons for Change
5/17	12 – 14	Interest rate changes invalidated basic financial assumptions
7/15	3	New EPA regulation requires change in product formulation

The following pages are hints to help you with the plan presentation. Read through them. Develop a presentation plan.

Good luck!

BUSINESS PLAN

Major Steps to Acceptance

FIRST READING

Whether the plan is being presented internally or externally, the first reading is a major step. The plan must offer something that keeps the reader interested. Some things to keep in mind are:

1. Keep it simple.

2. Make it readable (grammatically correct, action oriented, short sentences).

3. Make certain it holds together.

4. Provide an executive summary.

WILLINGNESS TO CHANGE

1. The plan is a means to accomplish objectives and is not the objective itself.

2. If there is something that needs to be modified, do it before making an in-person presentation.

IN-PERSON PRESENTATION

When the plan has passed the first step you will probably be invited to present the plan to appropriate decision makers. This may well be the make-or-break point for the plan. Remember to:

1. Have visual aids for critical segments of the plan

2. Prepare for pointed questions specifically in the areas of:

   a. The ability to make it happen

   b. The adequacy of the research and development behind the product

   c. The validity of the market research

   d. Your understanding of the business

   e. The financial projections and why they will work

   f. Negotiating the lower priorities to achieve the higher ones

FIVE PITFALLS THAT TRAP BUSINESS PLANS

1. Erroneous perceptions of the past from:

    a. Inaccurate narrative history

    b. Inadequate financial statements

    c. Ignorance of past mistakes

2. Inadequate forecasts from:

    a. Wrong methodologies

    b. Inadequate internal records

    c. Misunderstanding of effects of externalities

3. Unclear objectives from:

    a. Unstated priorities

    b. Unwritten objectives

    c. Objectives not matching mission

4. Lack of consensus from:

    a. No top-down communication

    b. No top-down push

    c. Varying individual goals

5. Inadequate controls from:

    a. Late or inaccurate reports

    b. Poor analysis

    c. No feedback

10 WAYS TO MAKE SURE YOUR PLAN IS A WINNER

1. Put it in a loose-leaf binder.

2. Have an established process for change.

3. Be sure everyone has a current copy of the plan.

4. Use the plan as a reporting tool in management meetings.

5. Have all relevant managers sign the plan's sign-up page (back of the first page—gives everyone equity in the plan).

6. Ask the *what if* questions about the assumptions made.

7. Have preliminary responses prepared for probable and/or critical events.

8. Write the plan as a selling document.

9. Target your audience in the executive summary.

10. Keep it short.

Appendix

ELEMENTS

Vision: _____

_____

Commitment: _____

_____

Timelines: _____

_____

Phasing: _____

_____

Contingencies: _____

_____

Reporting: _____

_____

Change: _____

_____

INTRODUCTION

BUSINESS PLAN OUTLINE

1. Cover Sheet
   a. Company name and/or logo.
   b. Business plan and year
   c. Names (perhaps with phone numbers)

2. Sign-up Page

3. Executive Summary
   a. Two pages
   b. What's in it for the reader?
   c. How many different readers?

4. Table of Contents
   a. Make it detailed enough to be useful
   b. Should be about one heading per page of text

5. Major Assumptions
   a. Economy
   b. Suppliers
   c. Consumers
   d. Competition

6. History Section
   a. Two pages maximum
   b. Focus on relationship to plans
   c. Major events

7. Philosophy

8. Definition of the Business
   a. Usually less than one page
   b. What business(es) are we in?
   c. What is the glue holding us together?

9. Definition of the Market
   a. Consider buyers and sellers
   b. Can use strategic factors analysis to help describe sellers (competitive analysis)
   c. Describe buyers demographically, psychographically, and by distribution channel

10. Description of Products or Services
    a. Most emphasis on new ones
    b. Advertising information sometimes helpful
    c. No catalogs

11. Management Structure
    a. Show that you have the right people
    b. Quarter-page résumés
    c. Relate résumés to goals

12. Strategies, Objectives, Goals, and Tactics
    a. Longest section of the plan
    b. Strategies lead to objectives
    c. Don't forget operational objectives
    d. Objectives lead to goals
    e. Format to reduce writing and ease reading

13. Financial Data
    a. This is the plan translated to dollars
    b. Budgets
       —Capital items
       —Cash flow
       —Revenue and expense
    c. Cost-volume-profit analysis

14. Appendices
    a. Supporting detail
    b. Making it work
    c. Not a dumping ground for superfluous pages

INTRODUCTION

BUSINESS PLAN COORDINATION TIME CHART

Task		
1. Gather background data including plans, budgets, financial statements and performance evaluations for past five years (if available)		
2. Level 1		
3. Level 2		
4. Level 3		
5. Level 4		
6. Level 5		
7. Level 6		
8. Written presentation		
9. Oral presentation		

PHILOSOPHY AND MISSION

Who: _____

_____

_____

What: _____

_____

_____

When: _____

_____

_____

Where: _____

_____

_____

How Long: _____

_____

_____

PLANNING PROCESS ASSUMPTIONS

Since the planning process deals with creating outcomes by future actions, it is essential and necessary to make assumptions about events and circumstances outside the planners' control. These assumptions are critical to the plan.

Please complete this sheet for each key assumption you make.

Assumption	Probability of Assumption Being Violated	Impact if Assumption Violated

Return a copy of this sheet to the plan coordinator who will provide a copy to the next level planners.

PHILOSOPHY

Rank

____ Profits

____ Customers

____ Employees

____ Management

____ Community

____ Integrity

____ Growth

____ Planning

____ _____

____ _____

SUGGESTIONS FOR USE

Philosophy

1. The list of topics may not be complete. Add different topics if appropriate.

2. Rank the topics in order of their importance to the company. Compare your ranking with others and discuss the differences.

3. Working with others, attempt to assemble a master list of topics and rankings upon which you can agree.

4. Working with others, write a short statement about each topic. It might follow the form: "We believe that . . . ; therefore, . . ." It usually helps later in the planning process to have included the *therefore*, since it can provide something to act upon.

5. Test the statements produced by asking employees to read them and then describe what changes might be produced in their jobs by acting on them. If few changes are suggested, you have probably done an excellent job of communicating or else the statements are in need of reconsideration.

6. Order the statements by the ranks assigned in suggestion 2, print them, and distribute them to employees before requesting their participation in the planning process.

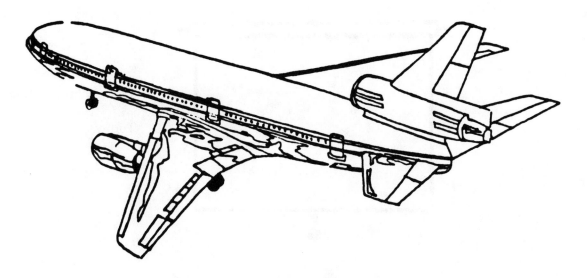

What Do We Do Best?

_____

_____

_____

_____

_____

_____

_____

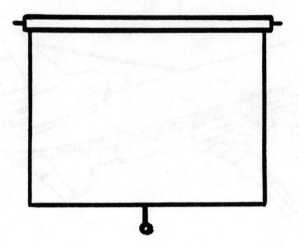

1904   Window Shades

Today _____

What Need Do We Meet?

_____

_____

_____

_____

_____

_____

_____

Whose Need Do We Meet?

_____

_____

_____

_____

_____

_____

_____

_____

WHAT BUSINESS ARE WE IN?

1. What Do We Do Best?

   _____

   _____

   _____

2. What Need Do We Meet?

   _____

   _____

   _____

3. Whose Need Do We Meet?

   _____

   _____

   _____

4. What Business Are We in?

   _____

   _____

   _____

SUGGESTIONS FOR USE

What Business Are We In?

1. Answer question 1, considering both:

    a. What do we do better than anything else we do?

    and

    b. What do we do better than anyone else who does it?

2. Answer question 2, considering needs at a basic level and not a need for product or service.

3. Answer question 3, considering not just with whom you may come into contact, but also:

    a. Who really derives the benefits or has needs met?

    and

    b. Who actually pays and why are they willing?

4. Answer question 4 by combining the answers to the first three questions. It may be possible to do this in one sentence. This answer may constitute your mission statement.

5. If your company is actually in several businesses, it is best to write a mission statement for each and add a statement describing the so-called glue which holds them together.

6. You may wish to add to the mission statement describing the path the business may follow while growing. Growth could be along present lines, or it could require considerable change.

STRATEGIC PLAN

Who: _____

_____

_____

What: _____

_____

_____

When: _____

_____

_____

Where: _____

_____

_____

How Long: _____

_____

_____

PLANNING PROCESS ASSUMPTIONS

Since the planning process deals with creating outcomes by future actions, it is essential and necessary to make assumptions about events and circumstances outside the planners' control. These assumptions are critical to the plan.

Please complete this sheet for each key assumption you make.

Assumption	Probability of Assumption Being Violated	Impact if Assumption Violated

Return a copy of this sheet to the plan coordinator who will provide a copy to the next level planners.

SWOT ANALYSIS

Strengths	Weaknesses
_____	_____
_____	_____
_____	_____
_____	_____
_____	_____
_____	_____
_____	_____
_____	_____
Opportunities	**Threats**
_____	_____
_____	_____
_____	_____
_____	_____
_____	_____
_____	_____
_____	_____

SUGGESTIONS FOR USE

SWOT Analysis

1. List the company's strengths. You might consider what you think are the primary internal reasons for the company's past or expected successes.

2. List the company's weaknesses. *This is not negative thinking.* One of the greatest opportunities for future improvement is in correcting these. If this list is not at least as long as the previous list, consider that sometimes a weakness is a strength that is overdone and see if that gives you some ideas.

3. List opportunities. These may or may not also be available to competitors.

4. List threats. Again, these may or may not affect competitors.

5. For each strength, consider:

   a. How can we enhance it?

   b. How can we protect it?

   c. How can we use it to our advantage?

6. For each weakness, consider:

   a. How can we eliminate it?

   b. How can we disguise it?

   c. What does it keep us from doing?

7. For each opportunity, consider:

   a. What prevents us from taking advantage of it?

   b. How could we best take advantage of it?

   c. How long will it likely remain available?

8. For each threat, consider:

   a. What is the worst that is likely to happen?

   b. For how long is the threat likely to continue?

   c. How can we eliminate or minimize its effects?

9. Fill the sheet out again for each major competitor. *This is very important. You aren't thinking strategically if you aren't thinking about the competition.*

STRATEGIC FACTORS ANALYSIS

Customer/Client _____   Product/Service _____

Companies	Rank					
	Price	Quality	Delivery			

Summary

_____

_____

_____

_____

_____

SUGGESTIONS FOR USE

Strategic Factors Analysis

1. Identify specific customer/client or a specific customer/client group. Insert in upper left corner.

2. Identify specific product/service to be offered. Insert in upper right corner.

3. Identify the strategic factors considered important to the identified group in suggestion 1. Enter these as column headings along with *Price*, *Quality*, and *Delivery*.

4. Rank these strategic factors in order of importance, and enter your numerical results into the column headings labeled *Rank*.

5. Compare answers with others and attempt a consensus.

6. List yourself as the first entry under *Companies*; then, in descending order of market share, continue with a list of your competitors.

7. Compare answers with others and attempt a consensus.

8. Insert numbers into the matrix indicating each competitor's ranking with respect to each strategic factor.

9. Compare answers with others and attempt a consensus.

10. Identify rankings which are likely to be subject to attempts at change or which may be likely to change due to economic environment factors. Identify direction of such changes with arrows.

11. Compare answers with others and attempt a consensus.

12. In the space provided, write a short summary of the above described situation.

STRATEGIC PLAN OF ACTION

With specific reference to your competitors, what do you most want to accomplish? (State the accomplishments as specific results.)

1. _____
2. _____
3. _____

What course of action will you follow to cause these to happen?

1. a. _____
   b. _____
   c. _____
2. a. _____
   b. _____
   c. _____
3. a. _____
   b. _____
   c. _____

THIRTY QUESTIONS TO ASSIST WITH STRATEGIC PLANNING

1. Who are our five major customers (or classes of customers)?

   a. _____

   b. _____

   c. _____

   d. _____

   e. _____

2. What are the common characteristics of these five?

   a. _____

   b. _____

   c. _____

3. Why do they buy our product?

   a. _____

   b. _____

   c. _____

4. Who are three potential customers (or classes of customers) who do not currently do business with us?

   a. _____

   b. _____

   c. _____

5. Why don't these three do business with us?

   a. _____

   b. _____

   c. _____

6. Are there any obvious ethnic, age, religious, gender, or other biases in our customer base?

   _____

   _____

   _____

7. What is our most effective sales channel?

8. What products are our three greatest revenue producers?

    a. _____

    b. _____

    c. _____

9. What products are our three greatest profit producers?

    a. _____

    b. _____

    c. _____

10. If customers could not buy what we sell (even from a competitor) what would they do?

Demographics—Who buys?

11. Are our products purchased primarily by any particular age group?

12. Are our products purchased primarily by any specific ethnic group?

13. Are our products purchased primarily by one gender?

14. Are our products purchased primarily within any geographic area(s)?

15. Are our products purchased primarily by any income level group?

16. Are sales of our product(s) tied to sales or use of any other products?

17. Are sales of our product tied largely to any occupational category?

18. What is the education level of our primary purchasers?

19. Who (according to the above categories) are the heaviest users of our product?

Psychographics—Why do they buy?

20. What are the benefits each class of customer (see above) derives from using our product?

21. Which *advertising* has been most effective?

22. Whose *endorsement* might cause a person to buy our product(s)?

23. What types of *packaging* have produced the most sales?

24. What is the buyer's *hot button*?

Channels—Where do they buy?

25. Which distribution channel produces the most sales revenue?

26. Which distribution channel produces the most gross profit?

27. What has been the greatest change competitors have made in distribution channels?

_____

_____

28. What has been the most effective change we have made in distribution channels?

_____

_____

29. Why was the change (in question 28) so effective?

_____

_____

30. Is there a level in the distribution link which can be eliminated?

_____

_____

LEVEL 3

CORPORATE OBJECTIVES

Who: _____

_____

_____

What: _____

_____

_____

When: _____

_____

_____

Where: _____

_____

_____

How Long: _____

_____

PLANNING PROCESS ASSUMPTIONS

Since the planning process deals with creating outcomes by future actions, it is essential and necessary to make assumptions about events and circumstances outside the planners' control. These assumptions are critical to the plan.

Please complete this sheet for each key assumption you make.

Assumption	Probability of Assumption Being Violated	Impact if Assumption Violated

Return a copy of this sheet to the plan coordinator who will provide a copy to the next level planners.

HISTORY QUESTIONNAIRE

To be completed by: _____
Completing these questions will help to show how we became what we are and why we are positioned to do what we have planned to do.

1. Date of company's founding. _____

2. Original founder(s) of business, name of business, location of business, and purpose of business. _____

3. Changes in name, location, and/or purpose, along with corresponding dates. _____

4. Major economic or environmental events which have affected company. _____

5. Dates and explanations of major additions to or divestitures of business. _____

6. Major obstacles and problems the business has faced. _____

7. Turning points, and causes of greatest periods of growth and profitability. _____

LEVEL 3

EVALUATION CHART FOR PLANNING

Areas														
100														
95														
90														
85														
80														
75														
70														
65														
60														
55														
50														
45														
40														
35														
30														
25														
20														
15														
10														
5														

Instructions: For those elements of which you have knowledge, mark the appropriate square to give a score which answers the question "How are we doing with respect to this element?"
© 1985 Professional Growth Associates, Inc., Tallahassee, FL.

SUGGESTIONS FOR USE

Evaluation Chart for Planning

1. Solicit suggestions for *Elements*. These should be problems (things that need fixing) that participants in the planning meeting may have control over.

2. Sort elements by *Areas*. Areas can be designated by discretion. The most common areas are products or areas of responsibility. It should be clear who has responsibility for each area.

3. Select four elements for each area and enter them on the chart. Do not use prejudiced words such as *bad* or *late*.

4. Copy the chart and circulate it to those who will attend the meeting. This should be done approximately two weeks before the meeting.

5. Collect the sheets and record on a separate sheet the highest and lowest scores assigned to each element. Copy and distribute this sheet at the meeting.

6. Discuss each element by allowing one minute each to the persons assigning the lowest and highest scores. Next, allow additional comments (limited to one minute) from others who assigned scores—provided they have something to add.

7. Ask the person who assigned the lowest score, "What would you have to see before you could change your score to be five points higher than the highest score?"

8. Record the answer.

9. Move to the next element.

LEVEL 3

WHERE ARE WE?

To be completed by: _____

1. Why are we in business?

   _____

2. What business are we in?

   _____

3. Where are we in the life cycle of the industry?

   _____

4. Where are we in the life cycle of the company?

   _____

5. How did we get here?

   _____

   a. Narrative background of major events

   _____

   b. Historical financial information

   _____

6. What market factors affect us?

   _____

   a. Input side

   • Personnel

   _____

   • Materials

   _____

- Financing

  _____

- Equipment

  _____

b. Output side
   - Primary customers

     _____

   - Secondary customers

     _____

7. What internal factors affect us?

   _____

   a. Our strengths

      _____

   b. Our weaknesses

      _____

8. What other external factors affect us?

   _____

   a. Regulation

      _____

   b. Legislation

      _____

   c. Competition

      _____

LEVEL 3

WHERE ARE WE GOING?

To be completed by: _____

1. Who are the *we* referred to above?

   _____

2. What alternatives are available to us?

   _____

3. Consider the critical issues such as:

   a. Desired rate of growth

      _____

   b. Desired rate of profitability

      _____

   c. Desired public image

      _____

   d. New markets

      _____

   e. New products

      _____

   f. Availability of financing

      _____

   g. Capability of personnel

      _____

   h. Adequacy of plant and equipment

      _____

4. Where will our strengths take us?

   _____

5. What are our priorities?

   _____

STATUS QUO QUESTIONNAIRE

To be completed by: _____

1. If the company operates in the coming year in the same manner as this year, identify those areas under your budgeting control (budget lines) which:

   _____

   a. Must be increased

   _____

   b. Could stay the same

   _____

   c. Are targets for cost reductions

   _____

2. Again assuming the present methods of operations:

   a. Identify two conditions over which you have little control that keep your area from making a greater profit contribution.

   _____

   _____

   b. State two changes which you have (or can get) authority to change that should make your area more profitable.

   _____

   _____

   c. By what date(s) could the above changes reasonably be made?

   _____

   _____

HOW DO WE GET THERE?

To be completed by: _____

1. What alternative courses are available to us?

   _____

2. What are the pros and cons of each alternative?

   _____

3. Which alternatives match up with our resources and our strengths (path of least resistance)?

   _____

4. What option(s) gives us the greatest future advantage?

   _____

5. Which objective is first priority?

   _____

6. Who will be responsible for each identified course of action?

   _____

7. What time frames should each have?

   _____

8. What is the biggest stumbling block to achieving our objective? Can we break it into more manageable problems?

   _____

9. What major external economic events (devaluations, political overthrows, nationalization, recessions, etc.) do we foresee?

   _____

10. What major internal economic events (acquisitions, divestitures, retirements, product demise, etc.) do we foresee?

    _____

11. What will it cost—dollars, people, dedication, etc.?

    _____

12. Do we have checkpoints and evacuation routes established?

_____

13. Is it consistent with our strategic plan?

_____

14. Can we monitor and measure our progress?

_____

15. Does this fit our stated philosophy?

_____

$$\boxed{\textbf{LEVEL 3}}$$

HOW DO WE KNOW WHEN WE ARE THERE?

To be completed by: _____

1. Do you have a means to quantify your objectives and goals to the maximum extent possible?

    _____

2. Do you have controls built into the planning process? (refer to *Controls* section)

    _____

3. Can you describe the final product in sufficient detail so that others can clearly picture what you are attempting to accomplish?

    _____

4. Is the performance measure agreed upon?

    _____

PLANNING THE REPORTS

1. Show the plan
2. Show the actual
3. Show the difference
4. Show period and year to date
5. Determine when to require explanations
6. Explanations include:
   a. Who is responsible?
   b. What caused it?
   c. Should it continue?
   d. What is to be done?
   e. When will it be done?
   f. Should the plan be changed? When?

PLANNING THE CONTROLS

1. What is to happen?
2. When should it happen?
3. When and how will we know if it is going to happen?
4. When and how will we know if it has happened?
5. Can we divide it into a series of events?
6. Are there points where we can reconsider?
7. Who is responsible for making it happen?
8. Who reports?
9. Are reports quantifiable?
10. Are reports verifiable?
11. What are the tolerances?

INTERNAL DATA MONITORING

Item Monitored	Last Period	Current Period	Desired Pro Forma
Financial			
1. Profit Margin (Earnings/Sales)			
2. Asset Turnover (Sales/Assets)			
3. Capital Structure (Assets/Equity)			
4. Return on Equity [(1) × (2) × (3)]			
5. Accounts Receivable Turnover (Sales/Accounts Receivable)			
6. Accounts Payable Turnover (Purchases/Accounts Payable)			
7. Current Ratio (Current Assets/Current Liabilities)			
Operational*			
8.			
9.			

*Examples of operational data to be monitored might include:

- Backlog
- Down-time
- Rejects
- Calls received

PLANNING UNIT GOALS

Who: _____

_____

_____

What: _____

_____

_____

When: _____

_____

_____

Where: _____

_____

_____

How Long: _____

_____

_____

LEVEL 4

PLANNING PROCESS ASSUMPTIONS

Since the planning process deals with creating outcomes by future actions, it is essential and necessary to make assumptions about events and circumstances outside the planners' control. These assumptions are critical to the plan.

Please complete this sheet for each key assumption you make.

Assumption	Probability of Assumption Being Violated	Impact if Assumption Violated

Return a copy of this sheet to the plan coordinator who will provide a copy to the next level planners.

INPUT FACTORS ANALYSIS

Item	Information	Indicator	Source
Personnel: • Management • Technical • Supervisory • Production • Support			
Financing: • Long-term Debt • Long-term Equity • Short-term			
Materials:			
Equipment:			

INPUT FACTOR ANALYSIS INSTRUCTIONS

This sheet is to help you determine information you may need to properly develop your planning unit goals. In the left column labeled *Item* are listed the input factors of production: *Personnel*, *Financing*, *Materials*, and *Equipment* (sometimes called men, money, materials, and machines). We have listed some generic subfactors under the first two.

Consider the following as an example:

Item	Information	Indicator	Source
Technical Personnel	Availability of people in our area with qualifications for entry-level repair jobs	Number of people graduating with AA or BA degrees in Computer Science	Placement offices of the following schools:

Choose the most significant factors of production to you. Then complete this sheet as in the above example. Assign someone the task of gathering the required information.

LEVEL 4

Planning Unit _____

To be completed by: _____

INPUT FACTORS ANTICIPATION

Item _____

Annual Quantity _____

Seasonal Variations _____

Acceptable Substitute _____

_____

	Sources	
	Primary:	Secondary:
Price Range		
Lead Time		
Availability		

Anticipated Effects of Using Secondary Source or Substitute:

Costs _____

Quality _____

Sales/Marketing _____

Production _____

Personnel _____

_____

INPUT FACTORS ANTICIPATION INSTRUCTIONS

This sheet is most likely to be completed by those with purchasing responsibility. While it is quite detailed, it can be very helpful. You can use it to be sure that all appropriate people are notified not only of changes in raw materials or components used in the manufacturing process, but also of the anticipated effects of those changes.

_____
Planning Unit

To be completed by: _____

OUTPUT FACTORS ANTICIPATION

	Ours	Competitors				
		1	2	3	4	5
Price Range:						
Previous Year 19						
Current Year 19						
New Year 19						
Annual Quantity:						
Previous Year 19						
Current Year 19						
Next Year 19						

Describe Anticipated Changes in:

Total Market _____

Market Share _____

Number of Competitors _____

Product Substitutes _____

Advertising Levels _____

Customers _____

OUTPUT FACTORS ANTICIPATION INSTRUCTIONS

Having looked at the input side of the equation, we now turn to the output side. This sheet is simply a way of accumulating and systematizing your thinking.

You may want to provide copies of this to others in your planning unit and ask them to complete it and return it to you.

Planning Unit

To be completed by: _____

PRODUCT PLANNING RECORD

Product _____ For Year of 19 ____

		Year		
		Present		
1) Units Sold —Actual				
2) —Projected				
3) Unit Sales Price —Actual				
4) —Projected				
5) Unit Variable Cost —Actual				
6) —Projected				
7) Unit Gross Margin —Actual				
8) —Projected				
9) Total Revenue —Actual				
10) —Projected				
11) Promotion Expense —Actual				
12) —Projected				
13)				
14)				
15)				
16)				

Problems may be indicated by:

- Declining number of units sold

- Declining total revenue

- Declining margins

- Increasing price reductions to maintain sales

- Increasing costs as a percent of sales

- Increasing promotion expense as a percent of sales

- Significant variances between actuals and projections

PRODUCT PLANNING RECORD INSTRUCTIONS

The Product Planning Record will help you to accumulate and see trend information. For the present year and for the previous two years you can complete the *projected* and *actual* rows for each factor. For the next two years you can only do the *Projected* rows at this time (but of course you can compare them to actual later).

Blanks have been left at the bottom for factors you consider particularly important to you. Such things as *Number of Salesmen*, *New Territories Opened*, etc. may be placed here.

Review the information and see what trends are developing and what they mean.

Planning Unit

To be completed by: _____

SALESPERSON'S SALES FORECAST FOR 19____

Customer _____   Salesman _____

Units Projected

Product(s)	Quarter 1	Quarter 2	Quarter 3	Quarter 4	Annual
_____					
_____					
_____					
_____					
_____					
_____					
_____					
_____					
_____					
_____					
Totals					

- Summarize by division
- Summarize by product

SALESPERSON'S SALES FORECAST
INSTRUCTIONS

If you have responsibility for sales personnel you may want to use the Salesperson's Sales Forecast sheet. Require each salesperson to complete one sheet for each customer (or class of customer). Note that the form requests the salesperson to commit by quarter how much of each product he/she will sell to the customer.

The sheet should be completed in units, not dollars.

Obviously, this sheet helps to determine manufacturing flow, inventory levels, and cash flow.

Note that this sheet can also be used by service firms. The *Units Projected* will become billable hours and the *Product(s)* can be specific people or specific talents/skills.

Planning Unit

To be completed by: _____

SALES FORECAST SUMMARY FOR 19____

Units Projected

Product(s)	Quarter 1	Quarter 2	Quarter 3	Quarter 4	Annual
_____					
_____					
_____					
_____					
_____					
_____					
_____					
_____					
_____					
_____					
_____					
Totals					

LEVEL 4

SALES FORECAST SUMMARY INSTRUCTIONS

The Sales Forecast Summary is used to consolidate all of the information submitted on the Salesperson's Sales Forecast. After appropriate consideration (and adjustments, if necessary), it should be a good foundation for planning the production.

Planning Unit

To be completed by: _____

VALUE ANALYSIS GRID

Product/Service _____

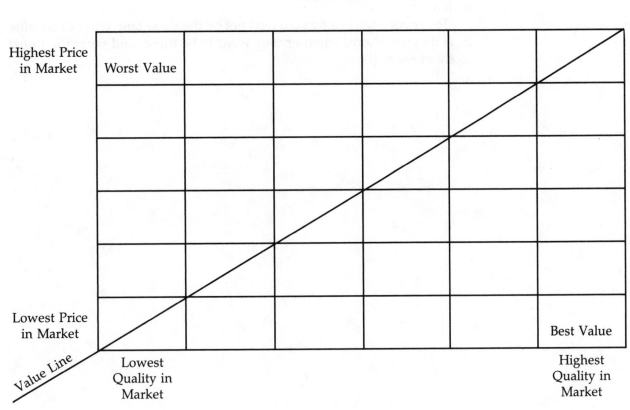

VALUE ANALYSIS GRID INSTRUCTIONS

We have chosen to put *Price* and *Quality* on the axis of the Value Analysis Grid. You may choose other factors if you deem them more important (Service, Components of Quality, etc.). Whatever you choose, keep the value concept foremost.

Choose a specific product or service to analyze. Determine where you think you are on the grid. Then place your strongest competitors on the grid. Also, look at the change in volume of business that each of you is doing.

For anyone (including yourself) not on the *Value Line*, try to determine how they got there, whether they want to be there, and what their next likely move will be.

┌─────────────┐
│ **LEVEL 4** │
└─────────────┘

PLANNING UNIT GOAL SHEET

Objective _____   _____

_____

Goal _____   _____

_____

Present Status (/   /   )

_____

_____

_____

_____

Resource Requirements

_____

_____

_____

_____

Responsible Individual _____

Estimated Completion Date _____

Concurring Managers _____   _____

Authorized Approval _____

Comments _____

_____

_____

© 1985. Professional Growth Associates, Inc., Tallahassee, FL.

LEVEL 4

OUTLINE OF

#	Goals	Expected Results	$

PLANNED CHANGES

Resources Required	$	Timelines			
		1st Qtr.	2nd Qtr.	3rd Qtr.	4th Qtr.

PLANNING UNIT GOALS

Who: _____

_____

_____

What: _____

_____

_____

When: _____

_____

_____

Where: _____

_____

_____

How Long: _____

_____

_____

PLANNING PROCESS ASSUMPTIONS

Since the planning process deals with creating outcomes by future actions, it is essential and necessary to make assumptions about events and circumstances outside the planners' control. These assumptions are critical to the plan.

Please complete this sheet for each key assumption you make.

Assumption	Probability of Assumption Being Violated	Impact if Assumption Violated

Return a copy of this sheet to the plan coordinator who will provide a copy to the next level planners.

GOAL ACTION PLAN SHEET

#	Tactics/Action Steps	Responsible Person	Status/Comments	Projections/Evidence of Completion	J	F	M	A	M	J	J	A	S	O	N	D

Goal _____

Report Date	J	F	M	A	M	J	J	A	S	O	N	D
Date												
Initials												

GOAL ACTION PLAN SHEET INSTRUCTIONS

This sheet is critical to the success of the plan. Up to this point the effort has focused on what is to be accomplished. Now you must show exactly how it will be accomplished.

You should call a meeting of your direct reports, those who will be assigned the responsibility of getting done the tasks that will accomplish your goals. Present them with copies of the Goal Sheet and of the Goal Action Plan Sheet (including the examples).

You must now decide what specific things must be done (*Tactics/ Action Steps*), who will get them done (*Responsible Person*), how you will know when they are done (*Projections/Evidence of Completion*), and when they will be done (*Timeline*). For the moment, leave the *Status/Comments* column blank. Put an identification of the goal for which this is the action plan in the lower left corner (by number or brief description).

Decide on this information with your reports and complete one form for each goal.

INDIVIDUAL ACCOUNTABILITY AND ACTION PLANS

Name _____

Position _____

Evaluator _____ Date _____

Approved by _____ Date _____

Individual Accountability:

Individual Action Items:

Measurements:

Performance Evaluation of Accountability:

( ) More than Satisfactory   ( ) Satisfactory   ( ) Less than Satisfactory

INDIVIDUAL PERFORMANCE EVALUATION

Name _____

Position _____

Dates of Review Period ____/____/____ to ____/____/____

Summary of Performance Evaluation:

(   ) More than   (   ) Satisfactory   (   ) Less than
        Satisfactory   Satisfactory

Too New to Evaluate:

(   ) Satisfactory Progress   (   ) Unsatisfactory Progress

Action Plan Summary: (Use additional sheets if necessary)

Strong Points _____

_____

Weak Points _____

_____

Plan for Development _____

_____

Evaluator's Signature _____ Date _____

Approved by _____ Date _____

Accountabilities Established:

(   ) Accountabilities have been established for the upcoming period.

Evaluator's Signature _____ Date _____

Approved by _____ Date _____

COORDINATION

Who: _____

_____

_____

What: _____

_____

_____

When: _____

_____

_____

Where: _____

_____

How Long: _____

_____

PLANNING PROCESS ASSUMPTIONS

Since the planning process deals with creating outcomes by future actions, it is essential and necessary to make assumptions about events and circumstances outside the planners' control. These assumptions are critical to the plan.

Please complete this sheet for each key assumption you make.

Assumption	Probability of Assumption Being Violated	Impact if Assumption Violated

Return a copy of this sheet to the plan coordinator who will provide a copy to the next level planners.

LEVEL 6

PLAN CHANGE PROCESS

This plan will be reviewed quarterly by its preparers. The review meeting will be held in the _____week after the end of the quarter. The meeting will be called and the location, time, and agenda set by _____ .

Included in the agenda will be:

1. A review of results obtained

2. A review of assumptions

3. A review of performance vs. plan

4. Suggested changes

Those having suggestions for additional agenda items should submit them at least one week before the meeting.

Changes approved in the meeting will be included in the plan book with changes to appropriate pages.

Date of Change	Pages Changed	Reasons for Change

Si exportada lo quieres pe y ensigelo no te detengas

Si exportada lo quieres pe y ensigelo no te detengas